Cannabis Underground Library

Seven Rare Classics

RONIN
Berkeley, CA
roninpub.com

CANNABIS UNDERGROUND LIBRARY
SEVEN RARE CLASSICS
ISBN: 0-914171-71-2
Copyright ©2000 by Twentieth Century Alchemist & Ronin Publishing

Published and Distributed by:
RONIN PUBLISHING, INC.
P.O. Box 522
Berkeley, CA 94701
roninpub.com

Printed in the United States of America

Distributed by Publishers Group West

Notice To Reader

Thanks to Stephen for the trippy mandala!
from *Amazing Dope Tales*, by Stephen Gaskin,
Ronin Publishing

Table Of Contents

The Cannabis Underground Library
Seven Rare Classics

The *Cannabis Underground Library* is a series of little underground classics from the long gone—and much longed for—"Sixties". It was a time when we were all so naive, still innocent and had all the answers: Free love! Free speech! Free smoke!

The seven rare classics found in *Cannabis Underground Library* are reproduced just as they were published—way back in those free days—with small illegible type and all!

Cannabis Underground Library is another of Ronin's Books-for-Independent-Minds which provides unusual, hard-to-find information in an accessible manner.

$2.00

A GUIDE TO GROWING CANNABIS UNDER FLUORESCENTS

By
C.E. Faber

Illustrations by
A. Faber

1

PUBLISHED BY FLASH POST EXPRESS CO

TABLE OF CONTENTS

SOIL

Cannabis needs a loose, well-drained soil for healthy growth. You can buy potting soil from nurseries or stores or you can concoct your own by using a recipe like one of the following consisting of garden dirt and materials you purchase in a garden shop.

3 parts soil
1 part perlite, vermiculite, or peat moss
2 tablespoons of superphosphates per gallon of soil
1 part soil

1 part perlite, vermiculite, or peat moss
2 tablespoons of superphosphates per gallon of soil

The reason you add perlite, vermiculite, or peat moss to the soil is to provide proper drainage and prevent it from packing down on the plant roots thus stopping them from spreading as they should.

In its natural state soil contains microbes that help the roots of plants break down nutrients. The dirt also accommodates molds, fungi, insects and other small animals which may be potential plant assassins. The potting soil you buy generally has been sterilized but it can become expensive if you plan to raise a number of plants. If you go to a field to obtain your soil you will at least want to pasteurize it if not sterilize it. By pasteurizing the dirt you will hopefully knock-off detrimental elements in it and save the good ones. To do this you wet the soil completely and put it in your oven at 150 degrees for one hour.

To sterilize soil you place it in your oven at 250 degrees for one hour and again it must be very wet when you bake it. Considering the hassle, the mess, and the possible odor of unnoticed baked bugs it might be best to go ahead and buy your soil if you're not going to have more than five to eight plants.

You may reuse the soil you have grown plants in before by removing as much of the old root system as you can and mixing in steer manure or a suitable high nitrogen fertilizer from a nursery. To avoid stunting your plants add only three-quarters as much fertilizer as directions say.

The pH of your soil refers to its acidity or alkalinity and it is something you will want to check. The pH is measured on a scale of one to fifteen with one being extremely acidic, seven neutral, and fifteen extremely alkaline. For Cannabis you want to aim at the neutral point of seven although the soil being slightly alkaline isn't as bad as it being acidic. If the soil is too acidic your plant will be stunted and the leaves become yellow due to the acid's hinderance of the roots' absorption of iron. If you added peat moss to your soil mixture you'll have to adjust the pH because peat moss tends to make soil acidic. This also holds true for a peat pot or Jiffy-7 pellet which you can start your seedlings in and which will be discussed later.

There is a kit on the market that allows you to determine the pH of your soil or you can use litmus paper. There should be instructions in the kit on how to treat your soil to attain the neutral point but if you utilized litmus paper a general guide for raising the pH is to add one tablespoon of lime per gallon of soil to get 1.0 change in pH. To lower it one point you add one teaspoon of powdered sulphur per gallon. If you overshoot the mark one way or the other don't worry because lime counteracts sulphur and vice-versa.

You should check the Ph of your water too, for if it is alkaline it will contain many minerals that go under the general title of "salts." The salt content of your soil and water has a great deal to do with good plant growth. Salts tend to build up around the plant roots and cut off the water supply when they crystallize. Evidence of salts is there being a white encrustation on the edge of your containers or on the surface of the soil. The best you can do in this event is keep the edges scraped clean and remove the top inch of soil every two weeks replacing it with fresh dirt. This will inhibit the salts from sinking down to the roots and strangling them.

CONTAINERS

When your seeds have germinated you should plant them in small containers loosely filled to the brim with soil. You can buy peat pots or Jiffy-7 pellets (follow directions with these) which have the attraction of the roots being able to grow through the sides making transplantation simple and providing a minimum of shock to your plants. You can also use yogurt or sour cream containers, half-pint milk cartons with the tops cut off, or plastic pots. When using food containers punch some holes in the bottoms of them so water can drain out.

To grow tall plants with a full array of huge green leaves you have to have good sized containers. Ideally they should be at least a foot deep and nine inches in diameter although more spacious ones wouldn't hurt. Too small containers cramp the roots with the result of your plants ceasing to grow unless you put them in larger containers. Your resourcefulness may be strained to find large containers for free or cheap. There are styrofoam pots available or you could ask a nurseryman where you might find some. I have seen plastic garbage bags inside doubled paper sacks serve quite well; they weren't much on looks but they did the job.

Be sure that what you use won't rust, and has good drainage. Be generous in punching holes in the bottom and lower sides, and an inch deep layer of pebbles in the bottom could only help.

LIGHTING

When you have given your plants rich soil in large containers the next prerequisite for healthy growth is adequate lighting.

Among all the colors in the spectrum, plants require mostly the blue and red light to flourish. Plants need blue light for the promotion of foliage, red light for stem growth and flowering. Although not as much blue light is needed as red, you will get plants whose development is tall without many leaves if excessive red and infra-red light is present.

I will discuss only the use of fluorescents at length because the ordinary incandescent light bulb is not satisfactory in growing superior plants. The reason for this is that incandescents emit too much energy in the far red (infra-red) part of the spectrum as a quick glance at Figure 1 shows. Even covering the bulbs with tinted cellophane or plastic is not sufficient for what looks like red or blue light to the human eye may not be the pure spectral colors the plants need. It takes expensive geletin filters to pull that off. Fluorescents by the use of special phosphors imitate these pure blues and reds superlatively so why hand a string of hot, one hundred watt bulbs to do what one forty or ninety watt fluorescent fixture can do better and more conveniently?

There is one flourescent used in office and household lighting that can be used in cultivating plants. It is the Cool-White fluorescent tube. The Cool-White runs a poor third to the Standard Gro-Lux and the Gro-Lux Wide Spectrum (WS). This is not because the blue and red energy it emits is inadequate, but because it does not emit an intense enough light for anything but slow growth. The Cool-White tubes should be paired with the Standard Gro-Lux or

4

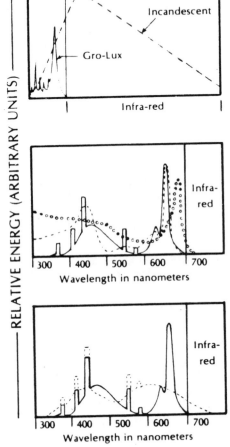

Figure 1:

Comparison between energy emissions of incandescent lights and a Standard Gro-Lux.

Figure 2:

Comparison between a Standard Gro-Lux, the spectral response level for photosynthesis, and the response level for chlorophyll synthesis.

——— Gro-Lux
- - - - Photosyntheses
ooooo Chlorophyll synthesis

Figure 3:

Comparison between the Standard Gro-Lux and Gro-Lux Wide Spectrum in spectral energy distributions.

——— Standard Gro-Lux
- - - - Gro-Lux WS

RELATIVE ENERGY (ARBITRARY UNITS)

Gro-Lux WS in which case their performance is considerably enhanced.

The most commonly employed fluorescents and the ones with which there is a wealth of information on are the Standard Gro-Lux and the Gro-Lux WS. Both supply blue and red light in suitably intense quantities to insure proper growth.

Figure 2 illustrates the spectral energy distribution curve of the standard Gro-Lux against the curves of the energy requirements for photosynthesis and chlorophyll synthesis of most plants. Photosynthesis is the complex process plants go through to grow and the basic molecule for photosynthesis is the chlorophyll molecule. The importance of chlorophyll molecules lies in their ability to trap energy from light and transfer it to other molecules that fashion the living cells of the plant from the inorganic materials they take from the soil and air. A green plant shows it has plenty of chlorophyll, is getting ample light, and is busy growing.

Different horticulturists have different opinions as to which of the two Gro-Lux lights is better. Figure 3 compares the energy distribution curves of the Standard Gro-Lux and the Gro-Lux Wide Spectrum. Blue light is found in the 435 to 475 nanometer range and red light in the 620 to 700 nanometer range of the spectrum. As you can see, more of the WS tub's energy is given out in the infrared portion of the spectrum (7.3 percent to be exact). For this reason it is not advisable to use solely the Wide Spectrum lights on your plants in order to avoid them becoming tall and scrawny. A good partner for the Wide Spectrum tube would be a Standard Gro-Lux or a Cool White. Two Standard Gro-Lux fluorescents would probably provide optimum lighting for Cannabis.

You should use at least two tubes for each row of plants to furnish a bright enough light for the balance between leaf and stem production. A single tube will probably result in your plants growing slowly and being scrawny.

In case you're interested, the cost of one forty-eight inch Cool-White tube is around $1.50, and the cost of the same size of Standard or Wide Spectrum tube is about $4.60. The fixtures are the main expense and a brand new forty watt fixture can run you anywhere from $13.00 to $17.00, depending on where you buy it. You might want to check a building supply surplus store to save money.

It is feasible to make your own fixtures but it might be simpler just to buy them. For instance you would need ballasts, sockets, wiring, electric cords, plugs, a wood plank to mount it all on, and assorted tools. If you are still curious then I suggest that you look in the electrical engineering section of your public library or ask at your friendly neighborhood electricians' supply store for exact instructions and materials.

The cost of running your lights on a month-to-month basis can be determined by substituting the appropriate figures in the following formula:

$$C = \frac{(W) \times (H) \times (30) \times (R)}{1000}$$

C=Cost
W=Wattage of your fixture
H=Hours per day you have the lights on
R=Cost of a kilowatt hour in your area

As an example: To find out how much one forth watt fixture would cost to operate sixteen hours a day at three cents per kilowatt hour (you'll have to check your electric bill to see the exact price of a kilowatt hour in your area) for one month, you do this;

$$C = \frac{(40) \times (16) \times (30) \times (.03)}{1000}$$

C=.58-cents per month

Most fluorescent tubes are rated to last fifteen thousand hours but the life of each tube varies. One way to know for certain that it is time to replace a tube is if the ends of it become dark.

If your fixture doesn't come with a reflector it is a good idea to make a simple one of tin foil so that more of the light is cast on the plants. It is also worthwhile to cover the walls near the plants with tin foil by taping the foil on them. If you have more than one fixture hang them as close together as possible – the more light you give your plants the better.

Very High Output (VHO) fixtures and tubes are available but they cost much more than the regular output tubes and fixtures. What the VHO equipment does is increase the intensity of the light by a factor of a little more than one-half. Excellent results in accelarated growth have been reported by people who have this equipment but as I said they cost more – the price of a fixture alone can be as much as fifty dollars – and this cost renders their use prohibitive to the average home grower.

The distance from the top of the plant to the light is very important. It is a law of the physics we live by that the intensity of the light diminishes drastically the further away from it you get. You must keep seedlings within an inch of the lights otherwise you'll end up with skinny plants as they stretch to reach the greater intensity found close to the tubes. Throughout their lives your plants have to be directly under the lights so they will grow straight and not waste energy bending to situate themselves more favorably.

As your plants get older it is best to keep the fixtures two inches above the plant tops. It is plausible to move the fixtures higher than this expecially if you will be away for a few days and want to avoid having the top leaves of your plants deformed and dehydrated by overlong contact with the tubes. Day-to-day, though, you should have the plant tops within two inches of the light.

The amount of light – measured in hours of exposure per day – you give your plants determines the length of time it takes for them to flower. Paradoxically, if you want Cannabis to flower early you give it less light than if you want it to flower some time in the future. A rough table of light exposure and flowering times would be: Twelve hours of light and flowering occurs in about two-and-a-half months; with fourteen hours of light flowering is in about three months; and with sixteen hours flowering is in about three-and-a-half months.

As you can see with the addition of every two hours of light there is a difference of around one-half a month in flowering times. You can decide when you want your plants to bloom by keeping this in mind. Incidentally with less than nine hours of light your plants won't get enough energy to grow well.

Besides the amount of light a plant gets there is something else that governs the flowering process. This something else is a chemical substance (probably a hormone) that is needed by plants in large quantities to bloom. The manufacturing of this hormone by the plants is done constantly but the storage or dissipation of it is regulated by temperature. At high temperatures a lot of the hormone is produced but a lot is also destroyed. It is during a colder period that the hormone can be made and stored by the plants till little by little the accumulation of the substance reaches a level where flowering can commence. Therefore, to aid your plants toward their blooming, a ten degree drop in the temperature during the dark periods is helpful.

Since it is the maximum amount of resin you are interested in your plants producing, and it is when your plants flower that this maximum is reached, you may want to let your plants obtain four or five months age by giving them twenty hours of light each day. Then you can encourage them to bloom by giving them twelve hours of light a day so that there is physically more of the plants to make resin.

Some say it will overtax your plants to expose them to light for twenty-four hours straight and others that it won't harm them a bit albeit they will never flower. Personally, I agree with the former opinion but if you choose to submit your plants to eternal day in an effort to wrangle more foliage out of them, don't rely on your fallible memory to regulate light and dark by trying to remember to plug in and unplug the fixtures. Invest in a timer that once set will leave you free of worry in this department.

The peculairities of your dwelling and the number of plants you wish to raise will dictate where and how to arrange your light fixtures. Your own ingenuity will be the limit on how you support the fixtures in your home. Bear in mind that the top limit of their height must allow for the height of the containers plus an allowance of five or six feet for the plants. You also have to make room for the expansion of the plants sideways. You don't want plants to be crowded or their leaves to touch for three reasons: First, so all the leaves receive light; second, to prevent the spread of insects from one plant to the others; and third, to allow adequate air circulation. A space of an inch-and-a-half or two inches between the containers should be plenty. This means that the fixtures should be hung so the containers over which they are centered have the two inch margin from a wall.

A suggestion on how to hang your fixtures might be for you to wrap a wire or tie a stout cord around each end of them under the fluorescent tubes and then up to eye hooks in the two-by-fours in your ceiling. These are then tied off to nails in the wall braces, or tied to the line where it is attached to the fixture. These arrangements hold up the fixtures and permit you to raise them as the plants grow taller. You may find that your plants grow at slightly different rates. If this happens array them with the shortest plants at one end of a row graduating to the tallest plants at the other end. It then becomes a simple matter of elevating one end of your fixture more than the other so that all the plant tops are more or less equidistant from the light source. This is easier than putting the containers on bricks to raise them.

You might want to hang your fixtures from pipes in your basement or attach them to the undersides of bookshelves. You could even build a custom designed stand or frame from which to suspend them.

No matter what method or manner you decide to employ, make sure the fixtures are secure and their weight well-supported, so all your efforts won't end some night in an avalanche of metal and glass that would be fatal to your plants and a definite bummer for you.

PLANT LOCATION

There are considerations other than available space to mull over when you are trying to come to a decision on where you will put your plants. Your plants need fresh air almost as much as you do but they need it for the carbon dioxide in it, not the oxygen. For this reason if you grow them in an enclosed space like a closet you should open the door for a couple of minutes each day so the plants can get new air to breathe. Establishing your plants in a room where you spend most of your time would be good for them in that they can inhale the carbon dioxide you exhale and you would benefit from the clean oxygen they give off.

Don't put your plants in a draft from an open window or an air conditioning/heating duct because a sudden change in air temperature could injure them. Also, if you live near a busy street the carbon monoxide pouring in a window onto your plants would be bad for them.

Avoid placing your plants near areas of heavy traffic in your house where you could accidently damage them by brushing against them or children in their innocent play toss a toy or fall into them.

Dogs and cats (especially cats) love to nibble on fresh vegetation. If you're not careful you could come home some time to find a plant or two denuded by a gluttonous pet who in your absence had resolved to fulfill his dreams of bucolic peace by indolent browsing. You might be tempted to make your return a more traumatic experience for your pet than you found it, so for everyone's sake, isolate your plants from your animals.

One more thing. Plants do prefer classical music to rock; violins to electric guitars, Stravinski to the Stones, so if you have a prediliction for rock it would be best for your plants to have them in a separate room from your stereo.

WHICH SEEDS?

The higher grade of Cannabis from which you choose your seeds the higher grade of plants you will grow with the provison that you give them proper care. The seeds you pick shouldn't be more than three or four months old as they tend to lose their vitality; germinating slowly, and producing poor seedlings if they sit around. You should also look over your selection discarding those seeds that are cracked, chipped, broken or dessicated. To store seeds for future endeavors you merely have to keep them cool and dry.

To germinate your seeds place a few more of them than the actual number of plants you want – they may not all germinate – in two inches of tepid water or in between five damp paper towels. Deposit them someplace where it is warm and dark and check them each day. Some of the seeds will germinate later than others and since these tardy ones would probably develop into weak plants, it is best not to retain those seeds that sprout after three days.

When a seed germinates, the seed coat will split and a white root tip timidly appears. Take it from the water or towels and plant it immediately one-fourth of an inch deep, preferably with the root tip pointing up. Cover it lightly with soil, don't tamp the dirt down.

TRANSPLANTING SEEDLINGS

Consider your plants to be seedlings until they reach three inches in height. The leaves will be small and the stem should be scarlet as though red ink or blood were flowing in it. As the plants mature the red turns to rust color and the stems will look striped, finally becoming mostly green. In their infancy a stem coloring of pale green or white should be interpreted as an indication that the seedlings are too far from the lights.

When you decide to transplant the seedlings have everything ready to go. To aid the plants in growing a more substantial root system bestowing extra support, you can bury the stems to just below the level of the cotyledons. When you do this you risk something called damping off, especially if the soil is unsterilized. Damping off is the result of a fungus attack on the newly covered stems which weaken them and can kill the plants. Rootone is a fungicide you can purchase and which will prevent damping off when you apply it during transplantation.

If you started your seedlings in a peat pot or a Jiffy-7 pellet, set the whole thing in the soil and cover it. The roots will grow through the sides of these containers without any problems though soaking peat pots in water for a minute before setting them in place softens them making it even easier for the roots to grow through.

If you used something else like the milk carton or yogurt container, water the contents so the dirt will be in a lump around the roots. Next place one hand over the open top with the seedlings' stem between two fingers being careful not to squeeze it between your fingers. Turn the container over and the clump of dirt will fall into your hand. If it doesn't come out the first time, tap the bottom of the container or press its sides to loosen the dirt and you won't have any trouble.

Set the root ball in the prepared excavation. Cover it and press the dirt down firmly so there won't be any air pockets around the roots.

CANNABIS SATIVA – THE PLANT

Cannabis Sativa – hemp, marijuana, grass, etc., etc. – is an annual of the mulberry family. If you like the color green and find beauty in symmetry this is the plant for you. It grows well in almost all soil conditions and in temperature ranges of sixty to one hundred degrees Farenheit. Being an annual means that it only lives for one season, growing, producing seed, and then dying, for once the flowering processes begin, the death of the plant is inevitable.

The major part of its life Cannabis simply grows sending out leaves in clusters known as palmate compounds. These compounds are made up of groups of three to nine leaflets. From the hollow main stem the first "leaves" seen after germination are the cotyledons. They are oval in shape and will die when the plant is about a month old. The next leaves are true leaves but there is only one leaf on each side of the stem. The leaves have serrated edges and their upper surfaces should be a dark green while the undersides will be a lighter green if the plant is well. As the plant ages, the leaf sets will consecutively have five, seven, then nine leaflets. In the case of polyploids more than nine leaflets to a compound is common. The stems on which the compounds sprout will be opposite one another early in the plants' life but later they will begin to alternate along the stalks.

At first it will seem like your plants are growing at an outrageously slow rate, more so since you will probably be looking at them each day. When they get to be about four inches tall there will be an explosion of growth that will keep you busy raising the light fixtures once a day as the plants surround themselves with a beautiful green halo of side stems growing from the intersections of the main stems and the compound leaves' stems.

When the plants have ceased to devote energy to the task of making stems and leaves the time to flower has arrived. Cannabis is a specie that has separate male and female plants although if the daylength is very short both male and female flowers can be found on one plant. Before they mature there is no real way to tell the sexes from one another.

The male plants are slightly less foliated than the females and their flowers are more inconspicuous. There are five greenish-yellow sepals and five pollen yellow stamen to each male flower. The flowers are in groups looking as though they hang upside down from the intersections (axils) of leaves and stems. Out-of-doors the pollen is borne to the females by the wind, but indoors you will have to do it by hand.

The main stem of the female plants sometimes becomes nearly invisible because of its leafy masses. The flowers are found in pairs in the axils of the upper leaves but frequently on spike of the pair will abort itself. The flowers consist of one erect pistil cupped by a calyx of fused sepals.

A great deal of resin is found in the hairs and glands of the female flowers hence the reason why the Hindus weed out most of their male plants and the reason why you should wait till the plants have flowered before you harvest them.

WATERING AND FERTILIZING

The easiest thing for most people to do is injure or kill their plants by literally loving them to death. Cannabis is a hardy plant that will survive in almost any environment providing the essentials of growth. Unfortunately, it is the home grower who tends to make environments unsuitable by a well-intended but over-zealous concern. This backfiring concern most often takes the form of overwatering or overfertilizing.

The ill-effect of overwatering is that it drowns the roots by not letting enough air get to them. The plants show this by the tips of the leaves turning brown. If you do not correct the condition by either increasing the number of drainage holes and/or cutting back on the amount of water you give your plants, they will remonstrate by dying.

Exactly how much water you give your plants is a hard question to answer. The main thing to keep in mind is that the appearance of the topsoil in the containers is not important. The wetness of the soil down by the roots is what you must accept as the gauge of the plants' water demands. You can test this when the seedlings are in their small containers by poking your finger a short distance into the dirt and if it is damp or wet, don't water. Generally, you water small plants every four or five days, but remember this is a variable.

When your plants are in their large containers you can push a pencil or your finger into the soil about six inches deep and should the pencil come up wet or muddy, or your finger detect dampness, don't water. As your plants become bigger they will be more than enough because your plants also absorb water through leaf cells when you spray fertilize them.

Here are some hints on watering you might want to observe:

Your plants will grow a bit faster if the water you use is at room temperature.

Let the water you plan to use sit in an opened container for twnety-four hours so as much of the chlorine in it as possible will dissipate. Chlorine is not good for your plants.

Water your plants thoroughly on one day, not a little each day. Maintain a calendar allowing you to keep track of days you will water and fertilize on.

The consequences of overfertilizing are even more immediate and disastrous than those of overwatering. The visible damage is yellowing of the leaves followed by brown spots on their edges or red"burn" spots on their upper surfaces. The leaves shrivel up and die, and in severe cases the plants may become stunted or die.

The best way to fertilize your plants is by foliage spraying once a week. The fertilizer is dissolved in water and using a clean Windex bottle or a sprayer you can get at a garden supply store, you generously spray a fine mist of the mixture on the leaves. The plant can make use of up to ninety percent of the fertilizer in this way, whereas a lot of the fertilizer goes to waste if you feed it to the roots via the topsoil. This latter method also increases the salt content of the soil. The best time to mist your plants is either just after the lights have been turned on or late in the "day."

Don't fertilize your plants until they are at least three weeks old. When they get older you can afford to do a complete job of fertilizing but when your plants are young and tender they really can't take it.

Use a high nitrogen fertilizer up to one month before you want the plants to flower. Nitrogen stimulates stem and leaf growth. When you want the plants to bloom use a low nitrogen, high potassium, high phosphorous fertilizer. On the label of the fertilizer there should be three numbers; the first is the nitrogen content, the second the potassium content, and the third denotes the phosphorous content. Ferti-gro, for example, is analyzed with these three numbers: 23-18-16. This means it contains twenty-three percent nitrogen, eighteen percent potasisum, and sixteen percent phosphorous.

Ra-pid-gro, Mira-gro, and Alask Fish Fertilizer are other good fertilizers but whatever brand you get it should be water soluble and always, always, always, add less fertilizer to the water than the directions say. About three-fourth as much as is indicated will keep your plants and you happy.

PLANT PROBLEMS

Diseases are a problem you don't have to worry about very much. If your plants are not crowded and they have proper ventilation and lighting, fungi and molds won't set in. In case of an onslaught from either of these two, a sprinkling of sulphur will get rid of them.

Insects are another matter. In the fields there are grasshoppers, slugs, snails, caterpillars, and animals of all kinds to menace your plants. Most of these find it impossible to invade your home but small insects are persistent and daring. Of all these insects there are four you have to maintain a constant patrol for.

APHIDS: Aphids injure plants by sucking the juices from stems and leaves and by their excretion of honeydew which serves as a culture for a black mold. They may also carry virus diseases which will do their share of damage. These insects are first found at the tender growth tips and buds. If they are not eliminated they will soon spread over an entire plant and then onto others.

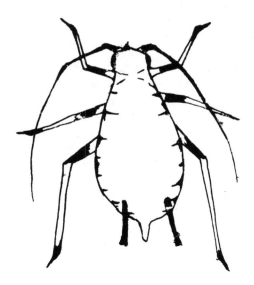

Adult: About 96 times larger than life.

Aphids are about one thirty-second of an inch long and green colored. Unfertilized females can lay eggs (sometimes these eggs hatch as they are being laid giving the impression they are live born) that develop very rapidly and, in turn, these aphids lay more eggs so that as many as fifty generations are born in a year. They reach sexual maturity in four to ten days and a female can lay up to one hundred eggs in her short month of life. With this prodigious ability your plants can be swamped in nothing flat by the multitudes.

You have two options when faced by aphids; go organic and use the aphids' natural enemies the ladybud and the praying mantis, or spray with insecticides.

Let us asume you choose the first alternative and that you prefer the cheerfully colorful alertness of the ladybug to the ominous green pose of the mantis.

Now you are faced with two problems involving the enlistment of the beetles to rid your plants of the aphids. First you have to find them and if it is not the right season, good luck! Second, when you have loosed your ladybugs among the aphids you'll have to admit that all the aphids aren't fools. Some of the brigands will start running like hell to escape their foe and cower in the soil of the container while their more dull-witted kin remain behind rapturously imbibing the juices of the plant as the hungry beetles approach. When the ladybugs have finished scouring the plant they wil be sated and bored or desirous of more game, and in either event, will fly away. Then the aphids who have been hiding in the soil or the new born in the crevices of a bud, will make posthaste for a succulent spot and in two days your problem will have returned, forcing you to go ladybug hunting again.

Consequently, unless you are a conscientious objector to the use of chemicals, you might as well resign yourself and apply Malathion, Miller's Vegetable Dust, or Diazinon. No matter what toxins you use be sure it is USDA registered and will oxidize before you harvest the plants. Wait at least ten days for the poison to oxidize before enjoying so you won't be a victim of it too. Be sure, too, that the room is well-ventilated or take your plants outside when you spray or dust so you don't get ill.

WHITE-FLIES: White-flies injure plants by puncturing the leaves to drink the juice and execreting honeydew. The adult white-flies resemble small moths with a white, powdery wax covering their wings and backs. The larvae are tiny green ovals found on the underside of leaves. They do not reproduce quickly and are not much of a danger to your plants if you catch them in time.

Adult: About 10 times life size.

There are natural enemies of the white-flies but they are extremely small and elusive hymenoptera; impractical for the home grower to try to use. Malathion, a summer-oil emulsion, nicotine-sulphate solutions, and soap solutions can be applied to the bottom of leaves generously once a week for two or three weeks in a row to rid your plants of these pests.

MEALYBUGS: These are wingless insects about one-fifth of an inch long, oval in shape, and covered with a white powder. They feed on plant juices they extract from the plants' veins causing the leaves to wilt and fall off. The eggs are laid in sack-like bunches with three to six hundred eggs to a sack.

Adult: About six times life size.

If you find them before they spread you can scrape them off the leaves and stems but if they persist you'll have to spray with Malathion two or three times at ten day intervals.

TWO SPOTTED SPIDER-MITES: These insects are the biggest threat to your plants along with aphids. They feed in the same manner as the preceding pests causing the leaves to turn a stippled grey-yellow, then brown and eventually falling off. The plant will become stunted and die.

The mites vary in color from red to yellowish to green to black and are so miniscule – one-fiftieth of an inch long – that it takes a magnifying glass to see them clearly. On the underside of the leaves small dots of silver are the webs to which the eggs are attached. If uncontrolled the mites will swathe the whole plant with this webbing. These webs may be the first real indication you find of the mites' presence. They multiply and spread like wildfire. To give you an idea of how fast this is, one female, at a constant eighty degrees room temperature, can give rise through succeeding generations to over thirteen million mites in one month.

In addition to this astronomical birthrate the little beasts are usually resistant to toxins and it will take repeated sprayings of Malathion or Diazinon to be certain your plants are free of them. The repeated sprayings are to take care of any larvae that may hatch from eggs already laid. There are no known natural enemies of the spider-mites.

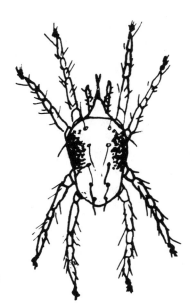

Adult: about 150 times larger than life.

PRUNING AND PROPAGATING

When you prune your plant it will become wider rather than taller. This is useful when you are growing platns in a place where there is not much room for them overhead, like under bookshelves. Remember though, that you must grant the plants more elbow room so you can't have as many plants under a fixture as you normally would.

Pruning is a simple operation. When there are three or four sets of leaves out you take a razor blade or pair of scissors and cut off the top bud close to the latest set. Two side shoots, miniature main stems in themselves, will grow out. When these side stalks have three or four sets of leaves on them you cut the center bud from them and so on and so on. After a while you will have a bush with a really amazing amount of foliage on it. Always water and fertilize after pruning and not just before. You have to decide whether or not you will prune early in the plants' lives for if you wait too long to initiate the pruning your plants will get top heavy and fall over.

Besides planting seeds, there are two ways of propagating plants. You can air-layer a plant or take starts from one.

With a woody stemmed plant such as Cannabis you can air-layer without any trouble. First, tie the stalk firmly to a stake. Then with a razor blade make an upward cut almost half way through the main stem, midway between leaf sets. There should be at least three sets above the cut. Separate the sides of the cut with a broomstraw or flat toothpick and cover the incision with damp sphagnum moss. Cover the moss with plastic wrap and tie or tape the plastic at each end loosely. Continue watering and fertilizing the plant as usual and when you see roots in the spahgnum cut through the stem below the plastic. Take the plastic off and pot the rooting.

Taking starts is as simple as pruning. Below three sets of leaves make a forty-five degree cut clear through the stem. Pot thiscqpn-vaf ke a tent of plastic wrap over it to conserve moisture. Place it about nine inches below your lights until, in a little under a month, it will have formed new roots and bUN TMGGW.

HARVESTING AND CURING

RESIN: This is the key to the potency of your plants, the quality of the resin – the amount of Cannabinol or THC in the resin – is already genetically determined so there is nothing you can do about that. However, you can do certain things to increase the quantity of the resin in the leaves and flowers when you harvest your plants.

About two weeks before you begin your harvesting, you should raise the temperature of the growing room and stop fertilizing and watering your plants. If you have a sun lamp or heat lamp, place it four or five feet from your plants and turn it on for eight hours a day, in addition to your regular lighting. These measures are to induce more resin to come to the surfaces of the plants to retard moisture loss. The leaves should become sticky to the touch as evidence of the increased resin flow.

If you have a large batch of leaves with a lot of resin, you can try to remove that pure resin as a form of hash. To do this, wash and dry your hands, then rub a number of leaves between your palms for awhile. After doing this, rub your palms together without any leaves using a great deal of pressure and the resin will be formed into tiny balls that you can collect. It takes awhile but it is worth it. For those of you who are interested in less exotic products, you can cure your harvest in several ways.

To quick dry your crop you can put the leaves on a cookie sheet and put it into a warm oven (150 degrees) with the door of the oven opened slightly as though you were broiling meat. Look in on the leaves frequently and feel them to see how they're doing. You don't want them to become too brittle as they should be somewhat pliable and not completely dry.

An even faster method of drying is to place a layer of leaves in a frying pan over medium heat. Turn the leaves every so often with a fork until they reach the desired dryness.

The best way to cure your harvest is by slow drying it. This can be done by cutting the plants down and hanging them upside-down for two days and then plucking the leaves off the stems. Or, you can detach the leaves from the stalks straight away and let them dry in the open for two days.

After the leaves have dried somewhat, place them in a Tupperware bowl or other tight lidded container and let them finish drying there. You should inspect the contents once a day to make sure no mold is growing on them. If you do find mold, scatter the leaves on a sheet of tin foil or wax paper to dry until the mold dies.

If you have a great deal of foliage to dry, then you might want to construct a drying box along the lines of the box Bill Drake shows how to build in his booklet, "The Cultivator's Handbook of Marijuana." Drying boxes involve some carpentry but are very good to cure your bumper crops.

Refrigerating your stash will help it maintain its potency and freshness longer than if you store it at room temperature. Pack it tightly in plastic bags, or to save space, roll it all up and tuck the bags in the back of your refrigerator or freezer.

For fun things to do with your harvest I would refer you to, *A Child's Garden of Grass*, by Jack S. Margolis and Richard Ghlorfene.

ARTIFICIAL MUTATIONS

Polyploidism is a mutational result which is highly desireble in most plants. Plants that are polyploids have double the number of chromosomes usually found in the genes of their species. These plants have the attraction of possessing more and larger foliage, and in the case of Cannabis, being more potent than the genetic blueprints in the seeds they are derived from would indicate.

The doubling of chromosomes takes place when the spindle mechanism during mitosis is paralyzed which stops the movement of the divided chromosomes to their respective poles at anaphase. This forms a nucleus with twice the normal amount of chromosomes for when no chromosomes are allowed to to to the expectant poles no cell division takes place. What this all boils down to is the cells in the plants become much larger than they usually would with the result of thicker leaves and a greater number of leaflets per compound. The pollen and seeds carrying this new genetic message are larger too.

The easiest method of inducing polploidism is by the application of the chemical colchicine. By causing mutations yourself, you compress the thousands of years of dice-rolling Mother Nature takes to come up with a new strain into a simple procedure of a few minutes or hours duration.

Colchicine is found in the seeds and bulbs of the crocus Colchicum autumnale which you can get at a nursery. It is a prescription drug used in the treatment of acute gout, so unless you have gout you'll have to get colchicine by crushing the bulb, a garlic press is a good tool for this, and straining the resulting liquid through filter paper.

At this point let me digress for a moment and warn you about the dangers of colchicine. It is a very powerful poison and could kill you easily. Use rubber gloves when handling it and don't get it in your eyes or on your skin. If you do get it on yourself, wash it off immediately with soap and water. Keep the solution in a bottle with a tight cap, and as with all poisons, including your insecticides, don't leave it lying around where children can get into it. You can buy the bottle, filter paper, a pair of tweezers, and an eyedropper at a hobby or toy store where chemistry equipment is sold. Never use these things around the house for anything else.

When you have filtered the liquid from the bulb you have a fluid that is about 0.3 percent colchicine. This in itself is too strong, so you have to dilute it by adding a third of that amount in water to the filtered liquid, i.e. two parts colchicine, one part water.

Colchicine must be applied when as many cells as possible are dividing or when it can be stored in dormant tissue – seed coats – until the divisions begin.

There are two places where massive cell divisions arise; in the budding tip of a stem and in the seed just after it has germinated.

To apply colchicine to the stem tip you can either dip it directly into the colchicine-water solution or put cotton soaked with the solution on it.

To dip a plant you take it from its pot and wrap the roots in damp sphagnum moss. Cover the sphagnum with tin foil so the roots won't dry out. Making a support for the root ball, you invert the plant and submerge the stem tip in the colchicine solution for twenty-four hours. When the immersion period is over, rinse the tip with tap water and repot your plant. This is a relatively laborious system and one fraught with the danger of possible injury to the plant because of the excessive handling.

A safer alternative is to cover the bud tip with a small cotton ball held in place by some tape. Saturate the cotton with colchicine and leave it in place for twenty-four hours. Subsequent to this treatment the plant will send out side shoots. Pick them off so the tip will be forced to grow.

To take advantage of the rapid cell division when a seed germinates you wait till the root tip poling from the seed coat is one-eighth to one-fourth of an inch long then submerge the seeds in enough of the solution to cover them. Leave them in for twenty to thirty minutes. After the selected time has passed take the seeds out, wash them thoroughly under the tap and plant them.

To supply colchicine to dormant tissue you soak your seeds in the solution for eight, twelve, or sixteen hours. Rinse them when you take them out and plant them.

Colchicine is very hard on plants and seeds so don't be surprised if some of them don't survive. Those that do will at first have stem and leaf deformities and be slow growing. When the new cells eventually take over the deformities will disappear with the number of leaflets to a compound being as high as thirteen or fifteen and the growth will speed up.

Let me repeat that colchicine is a virulent poison. The residue of the solution – even from soaked seeds – is in the plants you grow, so don't smoke the first generation plants. There is no transitory pleasure worth the risk of illness or worse, death. All you want from your first polyploids is the genetic code in the seeds they yield. I would suggest that you grow your first plants in twelve hours of light so they will flower early. Male Cannabis plants bloom about two weeks before the females. When the sepal covers on the male flowers are fully distended and the anthers hang heavily coated with pollen, cut them from the stems and store them in a jar.

When the female flowers have bloomed get a small paint brush and dip it in the jar containing the pollen. Brush the pistils of the females gently so they receive the pollen. Now you wait for the female plants to look as though they are dying. Cut the seed pods from the plants and let them dry out. You should find your seeds within these pods.

Don't treat first generation or successive generations of polyploids with colchicine to try and develop more potent plants. Studies show that such treatments cause artificial polyploids to revert back to the cell structure of their original parents.

There is one other way of creating mutations and that is by using radioisotopes. The radioactive material you can buy is very weak but somewhat expensive. It comes in a bottle to which you may have to add water. If there is a pharmaceutical drug manufacturer in your town you might get it from them or you can write the AEC for information on suppliers. Tell them what you want the isotopes for and they can suggest which of the many kinds would be most effective.

Treatment with isotopes is about the same as with colchicine except that you apply them for three or four days instead of a twenty-four hour period. Inducing mutations with radiation is not as sure a thing as using colchicine but if you have an interest and the time you might come up with a completely new strain of Cannabis.

Your Notes

SUPERMOTHER'S

COOKING

WITH GRASS

$1.50

© 1971
Sunshine Manufacturing & Import Co.
San Rafael, California

33

SUPERMOTHER'S
COOKING WITH GRASS

TABLE OF CONTENTS

PUBLISHED BY:
FLASH MAIL ORDER
POST EXPRESS CO.
SAN RAFAEL, CA. 94902

© 1971

SUPERMOTHER'S COOKING WITH GRASS

Banana Coffee Cake

1 cup sifted flour
1 1/4 teaspoons baking powder
1/2 teaspoon salt
2 tablespoons sugar
1/8 cup grass
4 tablespoons shortening
1 egg, well beaten
1/4 cup cow milk

Sift flour once, measure, add baking powder, salt, sugar and grass and sift again. Cut in shortening. Mix egg with milk, add to flour mixture and blend. spread in greased pan, 8 x 8 inches. Cover with topping and bake in moderate oven (375 F.) 30 to 35 minutes.

To make topping, peel and slice 3 ripe bananas and arrange on dough. Brush with lemon juice and melted butter. Sprinkle with mixture made by mixing 3 tablespoons sugar, 1/2 teaspoons cinnamon, and 1 teaspoon grated orange rind.

SUPERMOTHER'S COOKING WITH GRASS

Brownies

2/3 cup sifted flour
1/2 teaspoon baking powder
1/8 cup grass
1/2 teaspoon salt
1/3 cup butter
2 squares chocolate
1 cup sugar
2 eggs, well beaten
1 teaspoon vanilla
1/2 cup broken nuts

Sift flour once, measure, add baking powder, grass, and salt and sift again. Melt butter and chocolate. Add sugar gradually to eggs, beating well. Add chocolate mixture. Add flour, vanilla, and nuts and mix well. Spread in greased pan, 8 x 8 inches. Bake in moderate oven (350 F.) 30 to 40 minutes. While warm, cut in strips and remove from pan. Makes 24 brownies.

SUPERMOTHER'S COOKING WITH GRASS

Butter Cookies

1 cup butter
Confectioners sugar
2 1/4 cup sifted all purpose flour
1 teaspoon vanilla
1/4 teaspoon salt
3/4 cup chopped nuts
1/2 lid of grass

Melt butter in small saucepan at low temperature. Add grass and simmer slowly about 1/2 to 1 hour. Strain butter* Add melted butter to 1/2 cup confectioners sugar and cream until light. Add remaining ingredients (except strained weed) and chill for several hours. Shape in 1 inch balls. Put on ungreased sheet. Bake at 400°, 10-12 minutes. Roll in confectioners sugar, cool. Makes 4 dozen

*By sauteing the grass in the butter, the butter will retain the resin of the grass, but there is no visual trace of grass in the cookie. The effect is great.

Caramel Butter Frosting

1/2 cup butter
1 cup brown sugar
1/4 cup milk
3¼ cups sifted confectioner's sugar
1/4 lid grass

Saute grass in butter for 1/2 hour.
Strain off grass. Add brown sugar to
melted butter. Bring to a boil; stir 1
minute or until slightly thick. Cool
slightly. Add milk; beat smooth. Beat
in sugar till of spreading consistency.
Makes enough to frost tops and sides
of two 8 inch layers.
Note: Excellent on wacky cake. (see
page 15)

SUPERMOTHER'S COOKING WITH GRASS

Corn Muffins

1/2 cup sifted flour
1/2 cup corn meal
1 1/2 teaspoons baking powder
1 tablespoon sugar
1/2 teaspoon salt
1/8 cup grass
1 egg, well beaten
1/2 cup cow milk
2 tablespoons melted shortening

Sift flour once and measure; add corn meal, baking powder, sugar, salt and grass. Add egg and milk and stir only only until mixed. Add shortening and blend. Turn into greased muffin pans or non-stick pans. Bake in hot oven (425 F.) 20 to 30 minutes, or until done. Makes eight muffins.

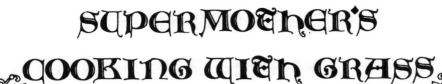

Crab & Oyster Gumbo

Melt over low flame:
  1 tablespoon butter
Stir in until blended:
  2 tablespoons flour
Stir in until golden brown:
  1/4 chopped onion
Stir in 1/4 cup grass for about 2 min.
Stir in:
  1 1/2 cups tomatos
  2 cans beef broth soup
  1 quart thinly sliced okra

Break into small pieces and add:
  1/2 lb. raw shelled, cleaned, shrimp
  1/2 lb. raw crab meat

Simmer these ingredients until the okra is tender. Add 16 oysters. Salt & pepper. Serve as soon as the oysters are plump.

Date Nut Bars

3/4 cup sifted flour
1 teaspoon baking powder
1/2 teaspoon salt
1 cup brown sugar, firmly packed
1/8 cup grass
2 eggs, well beaten
1 tablespoon melted shortening
1 cup finely cut dates
1/2 cup broken nut meats
1 teaspoon vanilla

Sift flour once, measure, add baking powder, grass and salt, and sift again. Add sugar gradually to eggs and beat well. Add shortening, dates, nuts, and vanilla; then stir in the flour. Bake in greased pan, 8 x 8 inches, in moderate oven (350 F.) about 30 minutes. While warm, cut in bars. Makes 2 dozen bars.

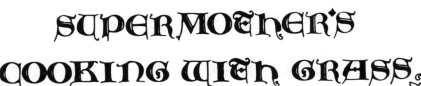

🎗 Pork Meat Balls 🎗

1 lb. ground pork
1/3 cup chopped onion
1 beaten egg
3/4 teaspoon salt
1/4 teaspoon paprika
1/4 cup grass

Combine ingredients with the hands until they are well blended.

Roll into 2 inch balls. Combine the contents of:

1 can tomato soup (10½oz)
Equal amount of water

Bring the liquid to the boiling point. Drop the balls into it. Cover the pan and simmer the balls until they are done (about ½ hour)

Pot Tea

Get ready a porcelain tea pot and a package of loose tea leaves, not tea bags, or remove the bag from the tea, leaving it loose.

Bring a kettle of water to a good boil, removing it from the heat as soon as it boils.

In the bottom of the tea pot put approximately 1/2 level teaspoon of tea for each cup of tea you are going to make (a little less if you dig weak tea) and add the stems and seeds which you have been saving, to it. Pour boiling water into the tea pot over the grass and tea, and cover. Tea pot might be stirred once or twice. Then go away and leave it alone for twenty minutes.

Shrimp Creole

First make Creole Sauce — fast way is to use can of tomato soup. 2 table-spoons butter & 1/2 cup finely chopped green pepper, onion, celery, olives and pickles.

Now — Melt in skillet 2 tablespoons of butter, add 1/8 cup grass. Fry for 3-4 minutes. Add 1 lb. boiled or canned shrimp. Stir and cook over flame for 2 minutes. Add two cups Creole Sauce and 1/4 cup dry white wine. Simmer for 5 minutes. If desired add salt, pepper and a few grains of cayenne. Serve shrimp with white rice.

§ Shrimp Wiggle §

5 tablespoons butter
1/8 cup grass
2 tablespoons flour
1 1/4 cup milk
1 cup shrimp
1 cup drained fresh peas
2-3 mushrooms
1 egg yolk
Dash salt
Dash paprika
1 tablespoon lemon juice or
sherry

Melt butter and add grass to cook for 4-5 minutes. Stir in flour. Gradually add shrimp, peas and mushrooms. Season. Lower heat and stir in yolk, permit to thicken slightly then add in lemon juice.

Serve at once on hot buttered toast or the "wiggle" may be in greased baking pan and covered with buttered crumbs — brown the top under broiler.

SUPERMOTHER'S
COOKING WITH GRASS

🔥 Spaghetti Sauce 🔥

1/2 cup onion, diced
2 tbs. olive or salad oil
1 lb. ground beef
2 cloves garlic, minced
2 8oz. cans (2 cups) tomato sauce
1½ tsp. oregano
1 tsp. salt
1/4 tsp. thyme
1 cup water
1/2 lid grass

In large skillet cook onion in hot oil
till almost tender. Add meat & garlic
brown lightly. Add remaining ingredients. Simmer uncovered about 1 hr. or
until sauce is nice and thick; stir
occasionally. Serve over hot spaghetti.
Makes 6 servings.
Note: 1lb spaghetti will serve 4 to 6
as main dish with sauce.

SUPERMOTHER'S
COOKING WITH GRASS

Veal with Sour Cream

1 1/2 lb. boneless veal
1 1/2 tablespoons butter
1/6 cup grass
1 teaspoon chopped onion
1/2 cup sliced mushrooms
1 tablespoon flour
3 tablespoons water or stock
3/4 cup sour cream
1/2 teaspoon salt
1/8 teaspoon pepper

Cut veal in cubes. Melt butter in pan and saute grass 2-3 minutes. Place veal in pan and brown. Remove meat only and put in baking dish.

In the butter and grass, saute lightly onions and mushrooms. Remove from heat. Stir in slowly flour, sour cream, salt and pepper.

Put meat in baking dish, pour in sauce, cover and bake in low oven (250 F.) for at least an hour.

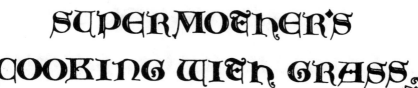

Vienna Pilaf

1 small can vienna sausages
1 onion, minced
4 tablespoons fat
1/2 cup uncooked rice, washed
1 cup canned tomatoes
2 cups boiling water
2 tablespoons grass

Cut sausages in small pieces. Saute sausages and onion in fat until lightly browned. Mix with rice, tomatoes and water. Season with salt, pepper and grass. Bring to a boil, stirring constantly; then cook over low heat about half an hour, or until rice is tender. Will serve two and perhaps one rather small being.

SUPERMOTHER'S COOKING WITH GRASS

Wacky Cake

1/3 cup oil
1/4 lid grass
Saute grass in oil for about ½ hour.
Strain and let cool.

1½ cup flour
1 cup sugar
1/2 tsp. baking soda
1/2 tsp. salt
3 tbs. cocoa (unsweetened)

Sift together into small baking dish
(6" x 9") Dig three holes in mixture
Into one hole add strained 1/3 cup
oil; into one hole add 1 tbs. white
vinegar, and into remaining hole add
1 tsp. vanilla. Pour 1 cup water over
entire mixture, stir *carefully* with
fork until blended. Bake at 350 for
3ᴜ - 35 minutes. Sift powdered sugar
over top while still warm.

Ancient and Modern Methods of

Growing
Extraordinary
Marijuana

Includes: Secrets of the
Ganja Farmers of India

by adam gottlieb

Ancient and Modern Methods of

Growing Extraordinary Marijuana

by adam gottlieb

Copyright (C) 1975 by Kistone Press

All Rights Reserved

COVER AND ILLUSTRARTIONS BY LARRY TODD

TABLE OF CONTENTS

INTRODUCTION — ABOUT MARIJUANA

Marijuana is a weed. There is nothing more to making it grow than putting the seed in the right place at the right time. In the hills of central Mexico many farmers simply scatter the seed upon the field in springtime and forget about the plants until harvest time. And what they harvest is dynamite grass. There the soil and climate are optimal for producing high potency hemp. On the other hand there are roadsides in the USA where marijuana flourishes for miles. But even the uptight local authorities are not much concerned about it since it takes three joints the size of cigars to produce even the mildest buzz. The difference between Mexican hill grass and the American roadside hemp is due mainly to the amounts of active THC (tetrahydrocannabinol) present. Primo Mexican grass may contain 3 - 5% THC while Midwestern roadside may contain only ¼ - 1%. This is not to say that Mexican grass is good while US grass is garbage. The author has had insipid weed in Mexico and has smoked incredibly potent stuff grown in a window-box in Madison, Wisconsin. It is simply the environmental conditions of most of Mexico are inclined to produce higher quality marijuana than are the conditions in much of the USA.

Another factor that influences both the potency and the quality of the high involves the balance of different cannabinoid materials in the plant. Marijuana resin contain several isomers of THC. The delta-1 isomer is the most prevalent and most potent. Some of this THC may be present in the form of THC acid. THC acid is not active, but much of it is converted to THC if the tops are properly dried after harvesting. Grass grown in hot, dry climates with a long growing season tends to contain more THC and less THC acid than the North American crops.

Northern grass also contains a greater percentage of cannabidiol than that from hotter climates. Ganja and hashish resin from the hot, dry countries contain only minimal amounts of cannabidiol while northern grass may contain as much as 33% cannabidiol in the oil extract. Although cannabidiol produces no high, it does act as an inducer and prolonger of sleep. This is especially true when it is taken with other active cannabinoids. It is because of the differences in cannabidiol content that some types of grass are stimulating while others produce grogginess.

It is also believed that the ultraviolet light which is more intense in the highlands of the more southerly climates may convert many of the less active isomers and cannabinoids to more potent forms. Laboratory experiments were conducted at the University of Illinois in which pure cannabidiol was exposed to UV light resulting in a 2% conversion to active THC.

It has been further noted that polyploid varieties of cannabis which have developed either through environmental conditions or through treatment with colchicine tend to contain a higher percentage of THC and less cannabidiol and other less desirable cannabinoids than do normal diploids.

2

BASIC MARIJUANA CULTIVATION MADE SIMPLE

Many cultivators in the USA go to great extremes to prepare the seed for planting. They soak the seeds overnight in water or wrap them in wet newspapers and incubate them in an oven for 8 hours. All this is unnecessary. Pre-sprouting does nothing to increase the percentage of germination, hasten maturity, or improve either the quantity or quality of the grass. All it does is speed up the germination period by a few days. Marijuana seeds may be either started in a seed-box or nursery and later transplanted to their ultimate location or started in their ultimate location. The only valid reason for starting the seeds in one place and transplanting them to another is to protect the seedlings from wind, late frost or the attack of birds. Any plant that is permitted to grow in the same place that is was started will not suffer the shock of transplanting and is likely to be healthier and more productive. We give instructions for separate germination and transplanting not because we encourage it but because it is sometimes necessary.

The soil should be similar to that to which the seedling will be transplanted. It should be a light sandy loam, high in nitrogen and potassium, with good drainage and an acid/alkaline balance between pH6.5 and pH7.5. Soil test kits are available at most garden shops or at Sears. Acidity can be increased by the judicious addition of aluminum sulfate. Alkalinity is increased by adding hydrated lime. Much has been written on how to tell if seeds are viable or not. Most methods are of value only to people who have excess time that they want to squander. In almost any lid of grass 80% of the seeds are viable. Often Colombian grass or grass that has been buried has a larger percentage of dead seeds. These are usually hollow and collapse when pressed between the thumb and index finger. It is best to simply plant all seeds. What comes up comes up. The choice of seed can make a difference in results. Seeds from superior breeds of grass are inclined to produce superior plants at least for the first generation or two. If you have a lid of dynamite weed, save its seeds for planting. If a seed box is used, its soil should be at least 4 inches deep. Seeds should be planted 2 - 3 inches apart and ¼ - ½ inch deep. Keep the soil moist but not soggy. If the soil is too wet, the seeds may rot. If the seed bed is out of doors and the nights cold, it is advisable to cover the seedbed at night with tarpaulin or glass. The seedlings should sprout within a week. Sometimes it may take up to 3 weeks. The seedlings should get full exposure to sunlight for the whole day or the equivalent in artificial light. Do not overwater the seedlings or they may develop stem rot and die. It is best that the soil on the surface be dry while that ½ inch beneath contains moisture. This can be accomplished by watering from the bottom rather than the top. The flower pot or seed bed can be placed in a pan of water until just enough moisture has been taken up. Never let the soil dry out to more than an inch below the surface. If started in the field, the young plants can be sprinkled or watered via irrigation trenches. Whether the plants are grown indoors or outdoors watering should be done in the morning hours. Seeds should not be sown outdoors until the rainy season has passed unless the seedlings can be protected from the excess water.

3

When the plants are 2 - 4 weeks old and 6 - 8 inches tall they should be thinned out if they are growing in their ultiamte location or transplanted to this location if they have been started elsewhere. The weaker plants can be removed. They can be discarded or planted elsewhere. The healthier plants which are retained should be spaced 2 - 3 feet apart in rows 3 - 4 feet apart. Rows should run north to south so that plants get maximum exposure to the sun. Be careful not to damage the roots when transplanting or thinning. Transplanting should be done in the late afternoon. The freshly thinned or transplanted plants must not be exposed to the hot sun or they will wilt. The plants should be well watered in the morning of the day that they are to be transplanted. So should the field in which they are being transplanted. Transplanting can be done in the earlier part of the day if the sky is overcast. In that case watering of the plants and field can be done about two hours before transplanting. If the plants are grown under artificial light, there is no need to worry about time of transplanting. This light does not have the wilting effect of sunlight. Prewatering, however, must still be done. Transplantone® or a similar product can be added to the water. It reduces the shock of transplanting and helps the plants to recover more swiftly. When lifting the young plants from the ground be sure that there is plenty of soil about the roots. If the plants are grown in flower pots, one pot 10 inches in diameter should be used for each plant. Do not use any fertilizer on the plants for at least two weeks after transplanting or thinning.

Marijuana needs full sunlight to grow profusely, mature properly and produce a high re. n content. If grown under artificial illumination, they should recei   ame light period as they would receive naturally - about 13 hours per day. The periods of light and darkness should fall at the same time each day, but it does not matter whether they coinside with the actual times of day and night outside. Artificial lighting should be supplied from a bank of wide spectrum Grow-Lux fluorescent tubes or an equivalent product such as Plant-Gro, Natur-Escent, Vita-Lite or Optima. Tubes should be spaced 8 inches apart. The tubes should hang just a few inches above the tops of the plants. If they are attached to a sheet of plywood which is suspended above the plants by chains or ropes on pulleys, they can be raised as the plants grow. The surface of the plywood behind the lamps as well as the walls and floor of the growing chamber should be either covered with aluminum foil or painted white to reflect and make available as much illumination as possible. A timer may be connected to the lights so that they will go on and off at the proper times whether you are there or not. Do not leave lights on continuously or for longer than 14 hours daily. This would prevent the plants from maturing and flowering. Sometimes plants may require supports. This is especially true of ones that are grown under artificial light.

Because tap water in some areas contains residues which increase the acidity of the soil the pH may alter over a period of time as these residues accumulate. It is wise to test the soil every month or so and adjust it accordingly.

When the plants are 12 inches tall they can be pruned. Lower leaf-branches that are losing their vigorous appearance can be broken off. The tops can be clipped back. This causes the plant to branch out and become more abundant in foliage. This clipping can be repeated from time to time until the flower stalks begin to appear. When they do you will be able to distinguish the males from the females.

Since the female is more potent and because pollination from the male weakens the female's potency, it is the practice of many farmers to remove

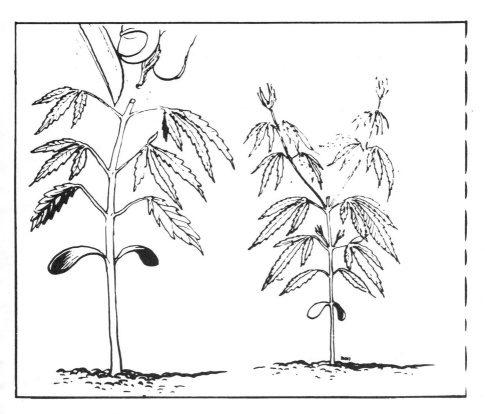

Clipping causes the plant to branch out.

all males before they blossom. These males contain some THC and can be smoked or consumed for a moderate high. When the female flower tops have begun to turn brownish or yellowish they can be harvested. They can be clipped off and dried in the sun or indoors at room temperature. Drying is sometimes done in an oven, but this is not advisable. When the leaves and tops are fresh most of the THC is present in the form of tetrahydrocannabinolic acid. It must convert to THC to have any effect. Slow drying causes the THC acid to decarboxylate to THC. Oven drying can be too rapid for this conversion to take place. In Mexico some farmers bend each flower stalk sharply at its base so that circulation is cut off at the top. The flower heads are allowed to dry on the plant for a week and then collected. The plants usually put forth a second crop of flowers after the first harvest. When this happens some cultivators will uproot the whole plant and hang it upside down for a week or so. This is said to prevent any THC in the tops from being drawn back by gravity towards the base of the plant and to cause some of the THC in the body of the plant to go to the tops. Harvesting should be done only on sunny days. The mature flower tops must never be exposed to rain or drizzle.

These are the basics for cultivating and harvesting decent marijuana. Now let us consider some of the things we can do to vastly increase the potency of our plants.

5

SECRETS OF THE GANJA FARMERS OF INDIA

For many thousands of years farmers of India have cultivated some of the strongest marijuana in the world. The most potent form is known as ganja and consists of the dried flowering tops of the female plant which have become coated with resin as a result of not being allowed to set seed freely. Although much of the superiority of the plants grown in these regions may be credited to the local climate and the probability that the strain of seed used is the consequence of ages of careful breeding (most likely *Cannabis indica* rather than our own *C. Sativa*), there can be no doubt that many of the cultivation techniques employed by these farmers greatly enhance both the quantity and quality of the active resin. A few of the practices described in this article are of dubious efficacy and are not likely to be worth the effort. Most of the information given here, however, is the result of thousands of years of experience handed down from father to son.

SOIL

It is universally agreed that Cannabis requires a light, well drained soil that has not been exhausted by previous crops. In Bengal a field is selected which has lain fallow for the previous two years or which has supported only light crops such as mustard or pulses during that time. The field, of course, is open to the sun and not shadowed by trees or nearby hilltops. First the field is ploughed and then liberally dressed with surface soil from the surrounding areas. After about a week this soil dries out and is treated with cow manure and reploughed. This is followed by harrowing. The ploughing and harrowing is repeated periodically until planting time. It is believed that the more ploughing, the better the crop.

In the Central Provinces such as Khandwa the prefered soils are *pandhar* or white soil mixed with ashes and sweepings from the village, and *mand* a light yellow alluvium permeable by moisture. Black clayish soil or regur is used when cannabis is raised for hemp, but is not favorable for producing plants of high potency.

In Khandwa, unlike Bengal and most other states, the same field is used year after year. Heavy manuring is not employed. Instead a mixture of household refuse, cow dung, and ashes is ploughed in at the rate of 16 to 20 cart loads per acre. In Berar white land is prefered. Black soil contains too much clay, is too stiff and has to be made lighter with heavy manuring.

PLANTING

In Bengal a plot of land is selected near the homestead as a nursery for starting the seedlings. The plot chosen consists of high, light sandy loam. To be sure of its dryness the farmer usually selects an open area where a tuberous-rooted grass-like vegetable called *matha* (*Cyperus rotundus L.*) grows. The land is not manured, but is ploughed three times before planting. Seeds are not sown on a rainy or even a cloudy day when rain is suggested. Wet ground rots the seeds.

When the seedlings are 4 or 5 weeks old and from 6 to 12 inches high they are transplanted to the field. First the field is ploughed, harrowed, made into ridges, smoothed and beaten down with the hand. The smaller plants are planted in higher, drier fields where they send down their roots quickly and easily and then grow up more swiftly. A month after transplanting the field is carefully weeded. Two weeks later the ridges are hoed down as far as possible without injuring the roots and well fertilized with oil cake or a mixture of oil cake and manure, and the ridges rebuilt over the fertilizer. Oil cake is the solid residue left after pressing oil from seeds such as olive or sesame. In the Himalayan area the seeds are often sown directly in the field. Chaff is then scattered over the field to protect the seed from the birds. In Punjab the seed is soaked overnight in cow's milk and water before being sown broadcast in the fields.

The cultivation practices in the Kistna district are essentially similar to those of Bengal. The crop usually follows millets, dry rice, coriander, tobacco, indigo or chillies, but sometimes hemp is grown in successive years. The nursery is made on the dam of a water tank and measures 6 X 60 feet. The soil is dug with a crowbar, reduced to a fine tilth and leveled. Seed is scattered upon the ground and covered by hand with soil. The bed is hand-watered as needed for the next two months. When the plants are two feet high the tops are removed and within a week they put out numerous side-branches. They are then transplanted to the field.

PRUNING

In Bengal the lower branches of the plant are removed 2 or 3 months after transplanting to the field. This helps to give the plant its pyramidal shape that brings the flowering tops as close together as possible and prevents the formation of ganja too close to the ground where it would get mud-caked. Immediately after pruning there is another ploughing and harrowing between the ridges. Then another application of fertilizer is given; after which the ridges are rebuilt. In Nepal, when the plants put forth fine down, the tips are cut off and the larger leaves are plucked. The plant is also shaken from time to time so that the down may fall off. This causes a large number of branches and fine leaves to be produced. These fine leaves get twisted and stuck together and are called *latta*.

Another pruning method in most parts of India involves roughly twisting the stem at the base of the plant. This stunts the plant's growth and causes it to produce more ganja. In some areas the flower heads are similarly twisted to prevent overbranching.

In Mysore a peculiar variation of the stem twisting technique is conducted. The one month old seedlings are transplanted into pits, each one foot deep, dug at intervals of 3 feet and well manured. The young plants are watered daily for a month of so. Then the stem of each plant is twisted just above the ground and the plant itself is bent horizontally to the level of the earth to prevent vertical growth and to induce the development of side-branches.

WEDGING

The twisting of the stem often causes a vertical split to occur near the base of the plant. Occassionally some foreign material is wedged into the split. This is supposed to increase the production of resin in the plant. More often than by twisting the split is made with a knife.

In the tributory States of Orissa the stem is punctured or cut and a piece of broken tile is inserted in the opening. In Gangpur cross incisions are made in the stem and a piece of opium or some other intoxicant is inserted. In the Kistna district the stem is split and opium or arsenic is tightly bound

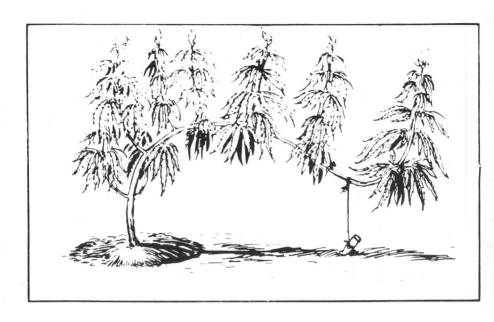

In Mysore plants are bent horizontally to induce side-branching.

A piece of wood, tile or other foreign material is wedged into the split at the base of the stem.

in the cleft. The use of opium in the split to improve the narcotic quality of the ganja is also practiced in Sind, Berar and Nepal. The Nepalese farmers also sometimes use a piece of clove or bhirosa wood in place of the opium. In some areas asafetida gum is used instead of opium for this purpose. These practices have their parallels in the USA where some growers now insert a thumbtack in the lower stem to stimulate resin reproduction, and in Oaxaca, Mexico where the technique of "crucifixion" is often used.

One of the most unusual methods of controlling growth is carried out in Burma. About a month before maturity, when the stem of the plant is about the thickness of a finger, the stem is split and a piece of wood is inserted. A basket - or sometimes a light earthen chatty - with a mouth about a foot in diameter is placed over the flower-bearing branches which are gethered together, thrust into the vessel and kept there for about a month. This prevents further growth of the plant and makes the flower heads grow thick.

EMASCULATION

A practice common to most of the provinces is the removal or destruction of male plants prior to flowering. This is done for several reasons: Male plants are not as potent as females and do not produce the resin that is necessary for it to be ganja. The male plant is believed also to produce a more giddy and less desirable high than the female. Removal of the male plants gives the female more room to grow. But the main reason for extirpating the males is that once the female has been pollinated by the male she will cease to produce resins and her potency will rapidly diminish. If a farmer in India is asked why remove the males, he is likely to answer: "What would happen if a ram were let loose among a flock of ewes?" The prefered form of ganja in India is that which contains little or no seeds. Such a product is similar in appearance to Sin Semilla marijuana grown occassionally in Mexico, but more resinous and potent than the New World product. We may take it on good authority that the seedless product is more potent than that which has been pollinated. It is obvious, though, that tops devoid of seed are a great convenience when preparing them for a smoke, especially when the high content of sticky resin may cause the seeds to adhere to the ganja.

In some provences a professional extirpator known as a *poddar* is hired to inspect the young plants and remove those which he recognizes as male. It is said to be a very difficult task to make a distinction at this stage of growth. We and most other cultivators of both the East and West find that there is no way to tell male from female plants until they have begun to send forth flower stalks. Most farmers are satisfied to wait until these stalks appear before attempting to cull out the males. Even when the *poddar's* services are used he must inspect the field once more when the flower stalks first show to make certain that no males remain and to remove any hermaphrodites (mutant females bearing male blossoms). Actually there is no need to remove the males until shortly before the first flowers open.

SPECIAL FERTILIZERS

Although the most commonly used manures are cow dung, sheep dung, ashes and household refuse, there are several unique fertilizers which many of India's farmers swear by for cultivating the highest potency ganja.

On the Punjab plains serpent excretia and swallow-dung are often used. In the Madras states the decomposed bodies of dead snakes is believed to be the finest fertilizer for potent ganja. Some farmers believe that there is a special advantage to placing the seeds in the mouths of freshly killed serpents and planting the whole thing. Farmers of Sind sometimes bury a dead snake beneath each plant or water the plants with dhatura-water (Jimson weed infusion) or huka-water (water from a water pipe through which ganja or charas has been smoked). Similar practices may be found in the Kistna district. Here decomposed serpent bodies and the dung of pigeons or other fowl are considered the best ganja fertilizers. Sometimes the seed or seedling is planted in the mouth of a dead dog or serpent which has been buried in a suitable position. Often water soiled from washing fish is poured on the ground about the plant. It is no surprise to anyone who has used commercial fish emulsion fertilizer on their plants that such experienced cultivators have found fish washings to be an efficacious plant food. One of the strangest methods of increasing the potency of cannabis plants employed in Sind involves attempting to get the plant poisoned by the bite of a cobra. When particularly strong ganja is required the cultivators of Bhopawar water each plant with ½ tola (90 troy grains) of opium dissolved in water. They also believe that transplanting the young plant to the mouth of a dead venomous snake (cobra prefered) renders greater strength to the ganja.

HARVESTING

The universal rule for harvesting ganja is to choose a dry sunny day. Harvesting is never conducted on a rainy, damp or even cloudy day when rain might occur. Much of the quality of Central Asian ganja is due to the dryness of the climate during the growing season. Cultivators of all provinces agree that after the plant has begun to flower in clusters and the resinous matter has formed rain spoils the ganja. The usual indication that the ganja is ready to harvest is that the leaves and flower-heads turn yellowish to brownish and the larger leaves begin to fall.

Much mention has been made of the narcotic superiority of the female plant and the weeding out of the males. This is not to say that the male plant is entirely useless. In India the carefully cultivated flower tops are taken for ganja or charas, both of which are usually smoked, whereas the leaves of the male plant along with the lower leaves of the female are harvested as bhang. Bhang is sometimes smoked by the very poor, but more often it is made into an intoxicating confection or beverage. For recipes made from bhang - or regular quality grass - see *The Art and Science of Cooking with Cannabis* by Adam Gottlieb, 1974, San Francisco, Level Press.

CULTIVATION METHODS OF
THE INDIANS OF OAXACA

Some of the finest Mexican marijuana is cultivated in the volcanic highlands of the state of Oaxaca in southern Mexico. Here the mineral rich soil, the hot, dry climate and the prevalence of ultraviolet light work together to produce grass of great potency and stimulating quality. In addition to these natural factors the farmers subject their plants to several operations which influence their chemistry and increase resin production. The philosophy of these farmers is that a normal, healthy plant which has grown under ideally comfortable conditions does not produce the best product for human use. To develop a potent product the plant must be tortured by environmental extremes, unusual pruning methods and the technique of crucifixion which will be explained presently. This philosophy is clearly rooted in the Christian-Pagan concept of spiritual ripening and salvation through suffering. Although the author is too much of a hedonist to appreciate the masochistic religious beliefs of Christians and other pagans, he must admit that when it comes to raising potent weed properly applied plant torture can be of great value. It is now well known that cannabis resins are produced as a protective coating against the hot sun and are inclined to be more abundant in hot, dry climates.

When the plant is just beyond its seedling stage the apical meristem (tip) is clipped. This tip is the site of the hormone and auxin synthesis in the plant. This removal of the source of these hormones causes the formation of lateral meristems (side shoots). The clipping or pinching off of the new tips is repeated once a week and causes the plant to take on a bushy, urn-like shape. Shoots which would normally fill the interior of the bush are also clipped. In its mature state a plant so treated will develop a thick, crystalline coating of resin. Constant clipping also affects leaf production and causes less of the large, broad, palmate leaves to occur and results in a predominance of verticillate, ball-like clusters of smaller, finer leaves in which the resins are more highly concentrated. These are similar to *latta* produced by the ganja farmers of Nepal.

Excessive pinching also alters the pigmentation of the plant. The changes wrought upon auxin production cause an accumulation of cyanins which give a reddish color to the plant. Panama red is the result of such treatment.

When the blood-like color appears the plants are crucified. This procedure is similar to the wedging technique practiced by the ganja farmers of India and the insertion of thumbtacks in the stem base now in vogue among many northern cultivators. In Oaxaca, instead of making one insertion in the base of the stem, two splinters of wood (toothpicks are perfect for this) are inserted at right angles to each other forming a cross when viewed from above. This causes an increase in the formation of active resins in the flower tops.

The Indians of Oaxaca have also succeeded in developing different strains of marijuana that are perfectly adapted to varied terrain conditions of the area. Excellent qualities of grass may be found both in the mountainous regions and in the valleys.

MODERN TECHNIQUES OF GROWING SUPERIOR GRASS

It is unfortunate that when a substance becomes illegal or taboo scientific research on the material usually comes to a near halt. Such has been the case with marijuana. Still, despite the biochemical dark ages through which we are passing, some knowledge of the plant's nature has been acquired. Most notable is the work of Sister Mary Louis Tibeau of the University of Wisconsin. Her discoveries regarding the influence of soil chemistry upon the plant's growth and resin production has been of great value to serious cultivators. The attempt of researchers Warmke and Davidson during World War II to improve the quality of hemp fiber in the male by grafting it to hops root stocks failed, but led to the discovery that a hops plant grafted to a marijuana root stock will contain cannabis resins. Experiments of individuals with secret indoor or outdoor farms have disclosed many other important facets about the nature of cannabis and what is best for its developemnt and potency. Also there have been several recent discoveries which apply to the improvement of any plant. We will examine here some of the techniques which are most likely to improve the quantity and quality of the marijuana harvest.

SOIL MINERAL CONTROL HYDROPONIC

The amounts of certain minerals in the soil affect the growth and chemistry of the marijuana plant at different stages of life. Abundant nitrogen during early development promotes growth and leaf production. Deprivation of nitrogen after most growth has been attained, but before flowering, stimulates the production of resins. Similarly, plenty of potassium in early life will promote profuse foliage and growth while too much in later life will inhibit resin production. Too much calcium during the plant's first stages will stunt growth and during later life will inhibit resin. Yet the plant has need for much calcium during middle life. Adequate magnesium during early and middle life helps to make plants tall and an increase of this material later on stimulates rapid maturity and resin production.

The ideal pattern of mineral distribution would be: high nitrogen and potassium, adequate magnesium and low calcium during the plant's first 6 - 8 weeks; sustained abundance of nitrogen, potassium and magnesium and increased calcium during the second 6 - 8 weeks; and sharply decreased nitrogen, potassium and calcium content, and increased magnesium after the 12th or 16th week.

The problem is how to control the soil chemistry in accordance with this pattern. It is easy enough to increase the calcium and magnesium at the appropriate times. But it is almost impossible to decrease the nitrogen, potassium and calcium contents during later life. When grown in soil this might be accomplished either by estimating the amount of these elements which will be depleted by the appropriate time or by transplanting to different soils for each life period. The first method requires continuous soil testing and accurate calculations. The second threatens the plants with transplant shock. The best way to control soil chemistry is to employ a neutral growing medium such as clean sand or vermiculite watered with a properly balanced mineral solution which can be replaced with a different solution at the proper times. In other words the best way to control mineral balance is through hydroponics.

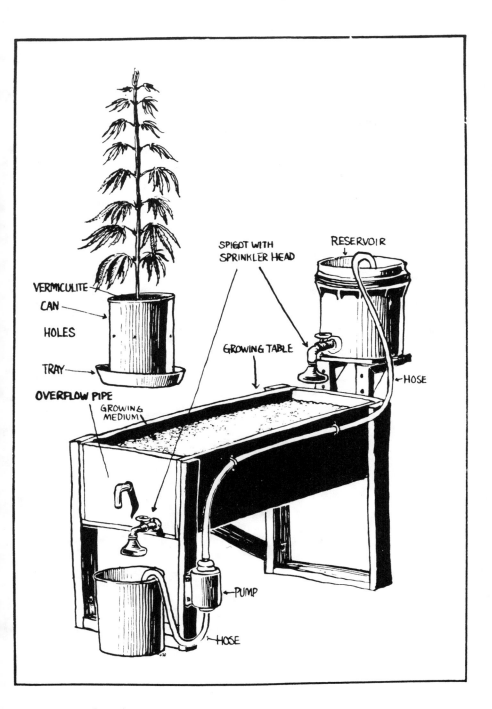

VERMICULITE
CAN
HOLES
TRAY
OVERFLOW PIPE
GROWING MEDIUM
SPIGOT WITH SPRINKLER HEAD
GROWING TABLE
RESERVOIR
HOSE
PUMP
HOSE

Hydroponics Containers

13

Hydroponics can be conducted outdoors, in a greenhouse or indoors under artifical light. It can be done in individual growing cans, or in a growing tank. If done outdoors a sealed wood or concrete pool about 18 inches deep can be used. The table or pool should be constructed of ½ inch thick exterior plywood and sealed with concrete, epoxy, tar or any other suitable waterproofing material. Zinc or galvanized metal should not be used unless they are coated to prevent toxic contact \ ith the solution and plants. Circulation is necessary to maintain aeration and to keep the mineral salts evenly distributed. If a can or a very small table is used, the solution may be drained daily and poured back into the container. General directions for building hydroponic containers are shown in the illustration above. Sometimes crushed rock, gravel, cinders, granite fragments, or brick chips are used as a hydroponic medium. Here, however, we are trying to maintain tight control over the chemical balance. The minerals present in these materials may upset that balance. If sand is used, it should be clean, coarse builder's sand. If beach sand is used, it must be washed thoroughly to remove salts and organic residues. Distilled or de-ionized water is used to prepare all solutions. Seeds are germinated in the growing medium with plain water which is replaced with solution #1 after two weeks. If cans are used and cultivation is done indoors under artificial light, the plants may occasionally be taken out into the sunlight - whenever it is safe to do so.

The following is a three stage formula for the growing solutions used for maintaining mineral balance as described here. Also included is the formula for trace mineral solution (TMS). This contains minerals which are required in small amounts throughout the plant's life. TMS is called for in each of the three growing solutions.

SOLUTION #1 (use after the second week for 6 - 8 weeks): Ammonium nitrate 9 grams, calcium nitrate 1.2 grams, magnesium sulfate 1.2 grams, potassium chloride 1.6 grams, potassium hydrophosphate 1.2 grams, potassium nitrate 1.2 grams, potassium sulfate 2.8 grams, TMS ¼ oz., water 1 gal.

SOLUTION #2 (use during the next 6 - 8 weeks): calcium nitrate 2.5 grams, magnesium sulfate 1.2 grams, potassium chloride 1.5 grams, potassium hydrophosphate 1.2 grams, potassium sulfate 2.8 grams, TMS ¼ oz., water 1 gal.

SOLUTION #3 (use during the remainder of the plant's life): calcium nitrate 500 mg., magnesium chloride 2 grams, magnesium sulfate 2 grams, potassium hydrophosphate 3 grams, TMS ¼ oz., water 1 gal.

TRACE MINERAL SOLUTION: boric acid 750 mg., copper sulfate 500 mg., ferric citrate 7 grams, magnesium sulfate 1 gram, sodium molybdate 500 mg., zinc sulfate 500 mg., water 1 quart.

Before introducing a new solution the table should be drained of the previous liquids and the growing medium rinsed with fresh water. These drainings and rinsings still contain much valuable mineral salts and should be recycled into the garden or compost heap.

MUTATIONS — GENETIC ALTERATIONS

There have been experimental attempts to mutate marijuana by means of X-rays and radiation. These energies affect the genes and chromosomes and result in alterations in the plant's characteristics. Unfortunately their work is chaotic and unpredictable and most always produce meaningless distortions. Far better results have been obtained by treating either the seeds or seedlings with colchicine, a toxic alkaloid derived from the autumn crocus [Colchicum autumnale]. Normal plants (diploids) have two sets of chromosomes per cell. Cochicine treatment causes a dividing of the chromosomes resulting in 3, 4, or 5 sets per cell. These plants are known respectively as triploids, tetraploids and pentaploids. Generically, any plant containing more than two sets per cell is known as a polyploid. These plants are larger, healthier and more resistant to disease than normal diploids. They have darker and more abundant foliage. The flowers, pollen grains and seeds are larger. The resin production is greater and the isomeric rotation of THC is inclined to be higher.

There are several methods of treating plants with colchicine. 1) When the plants are in the process of being transplanted the entire plant including the roots is dunked in a solution of 1 gram of chochicine in 1 liter of water and planted. This method brings good results, but many of the plants will not survive the drastic treatment. Those that do will be polyploids. 2) The seeds are soaked overnight in a solution of 100 mg of colchicine in 100 ml of distilled water (same dillution as for plants, but less solution needed) and planted in the normal manner. The seeds that survive treatment and germinate will be polyploids. This method is almost effective as treating the live plants. It is preferred because it is easier to sacrifice 60 - 80 percent of the seeds than the same percentage of 8 week old plants. 3) The ova of the female plants are dusted with powdered colchicine before they are pollinated. The seeds produced are planted. These plants will be dwarfs. Upon maturity the males are allowed to pollinate the females, but the females must be protected from pollination from any other male plants. The seeds produced by this mating are polyploidal and will develop into giant plants of great potency. As long as pollination from alien males never occurs all of the seeds produced in future generations of these plants will be polyploidal. 4) Sometimes plants that are in the vicinity of numbers of the autumn crocus (the source of colchicine) will mutate to polyploids. Autumn crocuses intercropped with marijuana may affect these changes, but the method is rather haphazzard and unreliable.

Colchicine is a very toxic substance. When working with it one should wear rubber gloves to prevent absorption through the skin and a breathing mask to prevent inhalation of the dust. Leaves that have been exposed to colchicine must not be smoked or consumed. The later foliage and flower tops are safe to use. So are the plants grown from treated seeds. Colchicine is often difficult to obtain. Names of chemical companies which carry it are listed in the directory entitled Chemical Sources USA, which is found in the reference section of most university libraries or can be ordered from Directories Publishing Company, Inc., Flemington, New Jersey.

There are reports of successful polyploidation of marijuana by dipping the young plants in chloral hydrate, but we have not verified this ourselves.

PLANT SHOCK

Some cultivators will insert a thumbtack in the base of the stem when the plant begins to send forth its flower stalks. This apparently shocks the plant either into producing more resin or driving the resins in the plant upward to the flower tops. It probably is the result of alterations in auxin synthesis. This is similar to some of the practices of the ganja farmers and the Indians of Oaxaca described earlier.

PYRAMID ENERGY

There have been many experiments conducted in recent years in which a mysterious energy generated or focused in pyramids has succeeded in improving various substances. Food placed in the volumetric center of a small cardboard pyramid (1/3 the way up in the middle) does not spol as rapidly as usual and tends to improve in flavor. Used razor blades placed in a pyramid overnight become resharpened. Detailed information on these phenomena and directions for constructing and using such pyramids can be found in the books *Psychic Discoveries Behind the Iron Curtain* by Ostrander and Schroeder, *Pyramid Power* by G. Pat Flanagan and *The Secret Power of Pyramids* by Schul and Pettit. Some vegetable gardeners have reported improvements in the quality of crops when the seeds are kept in the apex of the pyramid for several days before planting. There have also been reports that marijuana seeds treated in this manner produce plants of superior quality. There is an excellent chapter dealing with plants and pyramid energy in the book by Schull and Pettit mentioned above.

16

The
Super
Grass
Grower's
Guide

a handbook for
high power pot
farming

mary jane superweed

$1.50

Produced by STONE KINGDOM SYNDICATE

73

Super Grass Grower's Guide

1983

Stone Kingdom Syndicate

A MODERN METHOD OF GROWING SUPERGRASS

Hydroponics is the technique of growing plants in a nutrient solution without the use of any soil. This procedure was originally adapted as a controllable method of studying, individually or in combination, the effects of the various minerals involved in plant nutrition. Although it has not yet found universal acceptance as a standard system of commercial agriculture, hydroponics has numerous advantages over soil farming. Among these are: uniformity of growth, higher yields, greater freedom from weeds and diseases, more rapid and sustained growth, and saving of time, labor and mess. Also the balance of nutritional elements can be controlled with great exactness. Marijuana farmers can exploit this control to produce certain desirable results at different stages of growth—for example, good height and profuse foliage during early life, then high resin content and hastened sexual maturity before harvesting. Mineral control can also be used to influence the proportion of female over male plants.

TO BUILD A HYDROPONIC GROWING TABLE

There are numerous ways in which to build a growing table. Your choice depends largely upon the volume of farming intended. Here are several possibilities:

1.) For large scale farming a design similar to that shown in Illustration A will provide daily circulation of the nutrient solution with a minimum of human effort. This is accomplished with an electric pump, which can be purchased or salvaged from an automatic washing machine. Circulation of the solution is important primarily because it keeps the minerals evenly distributed throughout the table and furnishes aeration necessary to the health of the plants. The table can be constructed of 1/2-inch thick exterior plywood and sealed with tar, concrete, epoxy resin or any suitable waterproofing material. Do not use zinc or galvanized metal unless you intend to cover it with tar; these metals can be toxic to plants. A piece of wire mesh should be fixed over the spigot hole

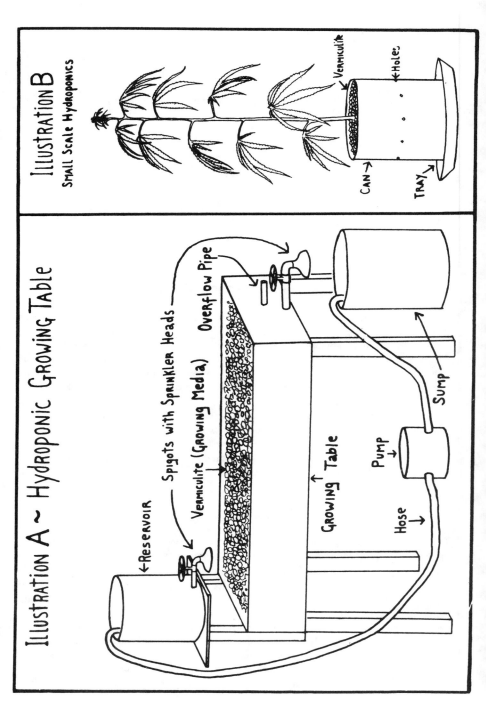

Illustration A ~ Hydroponic Growing Table

Illustration B
Small Scale Hydroponics

on the inside of the box to prevent stray particles of rooting aggregate from entering and possibly clogging or damaging the pump. The sprinkler heads on two spigots help further to aerate the solution. The hydroponic table is filled to about an inch from the top with Vermiculite, an absorbent insulating aggregate available at most hardware stores or lumber yards for about 60 cents a pound. Some stores carry horticultural grades of this material. Other common rooting media are cinders, granite chips, broken brick, fine gravel (1/8 to 3/8 inch), crushed stone and sand. The difficulty with most of these (especially brick) is that they may contain water-soluble mineral substances which could throw off the delicate chemical balance of the nutrient. Sand is good if it is neutral, lime-free, coarse textured and thoroughly washed. Nutrient solution is poured over the rooting media until it starts to come out of the overflow pipe. Because water is being constantly evaporated from the surface of the Vermiculite as well as being taken up by the plants it is necessary to add more nutrient solution every day or so. How often depends upon such environmental factors as temperature and humidity.

2.) For a medium size operation or one in which expenses must be minimized, the pump may be omitted. In this case the drained liquid in the sump is poured through the upper tank. Transfer twice the volume of water contained in the table, i.e., if the table holds 18 gallons and the lower bucket holds 3 gallons, transfer 12 bucketsful or 36 gallons total.

3.) For really small-scale farming any kind of two-gallon cans may be used: Punch or drill several small holes in a band around the half-way mark on each can. Fill cans to within an inch of the top with Vermiculite and place each can in a pie tin or some kind of tray to catch the overflow of liquid. Add nutrient solution until it begins to flow out of the holes. To circulate and aerate the nutrient place can in a bucket and pour half a can of fresh nutrient solution over the Vermiculite once daily. The overflow which comes out of the holes can be returned to the jug in which the nutrient solution is stored. The cans have the advantage of being light and portable so that indoor farmers can occasionally take their plants out in the natural light during safe and sunny hours.

NUTRIENT SOLUTION

There are several types of nutrient solution which may be used:

1.) Commercial preparations such as CAN-GRO or HYPONEX. Most of these contain an excellent balance of those minerals necessary for healthy pot plants. Check the label when selecting a brand to be sure that all of the minerals mentioned in this book are present. Use as directed and supplement those minerals which are lacking.

2.) Milorganite (commercially processed human manure) or sterilized animal manure. Mix one part manure with ten parts water. Allow to soak overnight, then strain through burlap. Unsterilized manure solution should be heated, held at a boil for five minutes, allowed to cool and then strained. It is best to add some chemical fertilizers to manure to be sure that all the necessary minerals are supplied. Manure solution should only be used if the growing tank is in a shed or greenhouse. It should not be used in the house. It is mentioned here only because so many people feel that it is important to use natural organic fertilizers. They may have a point in the case of crops raised for human nutrition. But it has been found that the production of high resin content grass can be better accomplished with a carefully programmed formula series.

3.) **Programmed formula.** The mineral balance in the growing table can be controlled to influence the plant at various stages of growth to produce certain predetermined effects during various periods of the plant's life. For example: oversupplying the plant with nitrogen throughout early life promotes abundant growth whereas nitrogen deprivation towards maturity encourages resin production. More about this as we get into our subject:

HOW TO GROW LARGE, FAST-GROWING, SUPERSTONING MARIJUANA PLANTS WITH HYDROPONICS

Select only large, dark seeds. Light green ones are less likely to succeed. They should be from a high-quality grass and preferably one which comes from a fairly tropical zone with long hours of light. These influences tend to produce temporary genetic alterations such as double and triple sets of chromosomes which, even under indoor and greenhouse conditions, may remain in the strain for several generations. The seeds can be started in the growing table. Place seeds two inches apart on top of the Vermiculite and cover with 1/4 inch of Vermiculite. Lay a dark cloth or plastic cover over the table. If you are employing any system of temperature control you may raise the temperature of the table to 100° F. for the first twelve hours (this stimulates rapid germination). Then let it drop and remain at 75° F. If you have no way to control tank temperature, you can soak the seeds for twelve hours in 100° F. water before planting. If any of the seeds have begun to sprout during this pre-soak, transfer them carefully to the growing table with an absolute minimum of exposure to light. When doing any transplanting (or plant surgery) it is best to work under green light. This lowers metabolic activity in the plant and renders it less vulnerable to shock. A green gelatin filter may be placed over any ordinary light source. One week after planting remove the dark cloth from the table. If possible set the room temperature at 60° F. while the growing solution in the table remains at 75° F. Keeping the growing media warmer than the surrounding air stimulates rapid growth and tends to produce more females than males. If you are using an artificial light source you can, temporarily, set the exposure cycle at 16 hours of light and 3 hours of darkness followed by 2 more hours light and another 3 of darkness; total 24 hours. The interruption of the night portion of the cycle contributes nothing to the successful growth of the plants, but it does stimulate hormones which cause a larger number of female plants to be produced. This can be accomplished with an automatic timer or manually. It does not require that you get up in the middle of the night to turn on the lights. If you are growing your plants in a closet or relatively lightproof room, the artificial day-night cycle does not have to coincide with that of the sun. Night in the growing chamber can be during the real day. During the germination period use plain water in the table. As more liquid is required to maintain the moisture level nutrient solution Formula A can be gradually added (see below). Two weeks after planting drain the water from the table and replace with undiluted Formula A. At this time raise the room temperature to 75° F. and let it remain there. Also at this time reduce the day cycle to ten hours and stop the nocturnal interruption. This puts the plants on the road to early maturity (about a week early). Persist with the ten-hour exposure for five days, then establish a "day" of fourteen hours. Weed out the weaker plants and let the remaining ones be spaced about 18 inches apart. Probably the only drawback with hydroponic farming is that plant tissues tend to be slightly softer than those grown in soil. Supports are recommended. These can be either canes or stretched cord.

FORMULA CONTROL

Formulae A, B and C contain the elements which are required in fairly large amounts plus an ounce of micronutrient concentrate which contains those which are required only in traces.

Micronutrient solution:

Boric acid . . . . 3 gm.
Manganese sulfate . . . . 4 gm.
Iron citrate . . . . 1 oz.
Copper sulfate . . . . 2 gm.
Zinc sulfate . . . . 2 gm.
Sodium molybdate . . . . 2 gm.
Water . . . . 1 gal.

(It is best to use pure distilled water.)

Because five-gallon water cooler carboys are ideal for storage of nutrient solutions, the following formulae are proportioned for that amount:

Formula A (to be used after the second week):

Potassium nitrate . . . . 6 gm.
Ammonium nitrate . . . . 45 gm.
Calcium nitrate . . . . 6 gm.
Potassium acid-phosphate . . . . 6 gm.
Magnesium sulfate . . . . 6 gm.
Potassium chloride . . . . 8 gm.
Potassium sulfate . . . . 14 gm.
Micronutrient concentrate . . . . 1 oz.
Water . . . . 5 gal.

Formula B (to be used after sixth week):

Calcium nitrate . . . . 12 gm.
Potassium acid-phosphate . . . . 6 gm.
Magnesium sulfate . . . . 6 gm.
Potassium chloride . . . . 8 gm.
Potassium sulfate . . . . 14 gm.
Micronutrient concentrate . . . . 1 oz.
Water . . . . 5 gal.

Formula C (to be used after ninth week):

Calcium nitrate . . . . 3 gm.
Potassium acid-phosphate . . . . 15 gm.
Magnesium sulfate . . . . 9 gm.
Magnesium chloride . . . . 9 gm.
Micronutrient concentrate . . . . 1 oz.
Water . . . . 5 gal.

These preparations are available, ready mixed, from Magic Garden Supply Co., P.O. Box 332, Fairfax, California 94930. $1 size makes one gallon of each solution with micronutrients. $4 size makes five gallons of each.

The hydroponic table should be drained immediately before introducing a new formula. Two weeks before harvesting remove three-fourths of the water from the growing table.

Do not replenish unless the plants start to wilt. If they do then add just enough water to perk them up. Water deprivation increases the production of resins and drives them to the tops of the plants.

The formulae given above are based upon the fact that marijuana plants have different mineral requirements at various growth stages and also that over- and under-supplies of certain elements can promote characteristics valuable to pot smokers. The specific relationships between the plant's physiology and nutrient chemistry are as follows:

Nitrogen – Abundance during early life promotes rapid leafy growth and female predominance, whereas a shortage of this element in later life stimulates resin production.

Potassium – Abundance during early life causes plants to grow large and leafy, mature early and be predominantly female. But too much of this element in later life can be harmful and will inhibit resin production.

Calcium – Too much in early life stunts growth; too much in later life inhibits resin. The greatest calcium requirements occur during middle life.

Magnesium – Abundance during early life causes plants to be tall, but too much will tend to produce mostly males. Increased amounts in later life stimulate early maturity and assist in resin production.

LIGHT

Although hydroponics works well for both outdoor and indoor growing, it is more likely to be used with the latter. If so, the plants may be illuminated either by filtered sunlight in a greenhouse or by artificial light. If you are constructing your own greenhouse do not use ordinary window glass- it filters out most of the essential ultraviolet light necessary for photosynthesis. Use greenhouse glass, which is available from any greenhouse equipment and supply house. If you wish to conceal your plants from the eyes of outsiders, cover the inside of the glass with translucent polyethylene or cast vinyl sheeting. Both of these admit the proper light; polyethylene is the least expensive of the two, but vinyl is the more durable. These materials may be located under "Plastics" in the yellow pages of most city telephone directories or ordered from Edmund Scientific Co., 600 Edscorp Bldg., Barrington, N.J. 08007. Be sure that your greenhouse gets a full day of sunlight. If it does not you should supplement with artificial light.

△

ARTIFICIAL LIGHT

For several reasons artificial light is best for growing high potency marijuana plants. Remember: abnormal growing conditions must be employed to produce abnormally powerful grass. There are many unique and interesting methods of artificial illumination which have been experimented with in the past. Some of these include the use of colored filters, sunlamps, mercury vapor tubes etc. These are thoroughly described in *The Complete Cannabis Cultivator* (see ad on back cover). After much trial and error under carefully controlled conditions we have concluded that the best low-priced light sources are the Sylvania wide-spectrum 40-watt GRO-LUX lamps, which cost $2.99 each at Sears

Roebuck, or any commercial equivalent, such as 40-watt NATUR-ESCENT tubes, available from Edmund Scientific Co., 600 Edscorp Bldg., Barrington, N.J. 08007, at $13.00 per set of four tubes. All of these fit standard fluorescent fixtures. Ordinary fluorescent GRO-LUX tubes predominantly emit light from the blue portion of the spectrum, but wide-spectrum lamps also emit a substantial amount of red light. These two kinds of light serve separate functions in plant growth. Blue light regulates respiration and stimulates leaf growth, especially during the seedling stage. Red light promotes later leaf and flower development. Many indoor farmers claim that for the most spectacular results you can insert ordinary fluorescents or blue-spectrum GRO-LUX lamps into the fixtures for the first nine weeks. After that switch over to wide-spectrum lamps. The outcome of this procedure, they say, will be lush foliage, early maturity, well-developed tops and high resin content. At the time of this printing our own tests with this possibility are not satisfactorily completed. If any adventurous experimenters care to try it, be sure to grow a control crop to test it against. We are always happy to hear about any unique experiments you have tried. Interesting letters will be answered with free gifts from STONE KINGDOM. When wide-spectrum lamps were not available a common practice was to supplement the red light deficiency with one 75-watt incandescent globe for every 40-watt fluorescent. Many plant physiologists insist that this procedure does not provide enough of the right kind of red light and more infra-red light than is healthy for most plants. Yet many farmers maintain that this practice works well and they continue to employ it. If you try it remember that most incandescent lamps begin to decrease their light output after 400 hours of use and should be changed at this time. Sylvania GRO-LUX lamps give full brightness for 18,000 hours, but turning them on and off shortens their life. When dark rings start to form at the ends of the tubes it is time to change them. If your growing space will not accommodate the 48-inch length of a 40-watt tube, they are available in shorter lengths with correspondingly lower wattage.

●

ARRANGEMENT OF LIGHTING

If you are growing your plants under artificial illumination, you will want to get the maximum efficiency from your light sources. Assuming that you are using a closet for a growing chamber, follow these instructions for best results:

1.) Line your closet walls with aluminum foil or at least paint them white. Dark walls absorb much of the light.

2.) Place the fluorescent tubes about four or five inches apart on a plywood board which has been cut to the dimensions of the chamber and covered with foil or painted white. Hang this in your closet on a pulley. As the plants grow you can keep the light bank about eighteen inches above their tops.

3.) When the plants get really tall the lower leaves will be too far from the light to receive much illumination. As soon as these bottom leaves start to wither they should be broken off, dried and smoked. Otherwise they will absorb much of the resin which is trying to reach the tops. At this time a few fluorescent lights may be placed along the closet walls to help illuminate the middle and lower foliage.

4.) The lights should not be left on for 24 hours a day. This could kill your plants, or at best cause them never to mature. During early life 16 hours a day is ideal. This will promote full growth and leaf development. But from the second or third week on 14 hours is best. Some growers who wish to accelerate maturity keep the light period down to 12 hours a day. Less than this can seriously inhibit resin production.

PRODUCING MOSTLY FEMALES

Although both male and female plants contain the resins which get you high, the female tends to be the more competent at producing these substances. For this reason—especially with small-scale indoor farming—it is desirable to have as many females and as few males as possible. And it *is* possible. Under normal conditions a seed is almost as likely to produce a plant of one sex as the other. During the seedling stage the balance of the male-producing enzymes against the female-producing enzymes decides what the sex of the plant will be. It is a balance so delicate that even slight abnormalities of environment can sway the decision. As was pointed out in the section titled "Formula Control," overabundances of nitrogen and potassium during early life tends to produce a high proportion of females. Conversely, an overdose of calcium or magnesium shifts the ratio in favor of the males. Drastically altering the normal day/night cycle can also influence the sex "choice" of a plant. Shortening the day span to seven hours causes plants to produce blossoms of the opposite sex. This phenomenon can be exploited to breed seeds which will have a genetic inclination towards becoming female plants. This technique is thoroughly described in *The Complete Cannabis Cultivator* (see ad on back cover). Since the seven-hour day must be maintained throughout the life of the plant a low resin count usually results. The interrupted night and programmed formula methods, however, if carried out as instructed, do not hinder the manufacture of resins.

SYMPTOMS, CAUSES, AND CURES
FOR MINERAL DEFICIENCIES AND OVERDOSES

If all of the elements listed in this book are accounted for in the formulae, there should be no nutritional problems. It is still wise, however, to keep an eye on your plants for signs of mineral deficiency or overdosage. The following is a list of symptoms, causes, and cures. Corrections for mineral deficiency must be applied with caution because of the delicate mineral balance involved in the programmed formula series. The assumption here is that all other factors such as lighting, water and air temperature are in proper order.

Yellowing of older leaves=nitrogen shortage. Since Formula A intentionally overdoses nitrogen a shortage cannot occur at this stage. But since the ninth week formula starves the plant of this element you will have to watch for deficiency symptoms. No more than two grams of ammonium nitrate per five gallons of nutrient solution should correct the condition without seriously disturbing the formula balance.

Older leaves slightly yellowed followed in a few days with dark grayish brown spots along the leaf edge=potassium deficiency. The program should supply more than ample potassium during the first nine weeks. If deficiency occurs after this time add three grams of potassium acid-phosphate per five gallons nutrient solution.

Yellowing of younger leaves which soon extends to the whole plant=sulfur deficiency. Six grams potassium sulfate per five gallons during first nine weeks or six grams magnesium sulfate after that.

Buds fail to develop and fine root hairs wilt=calcium deficiency. There should be enough in the formula, but if symptoms occur during the first six weeks add three grams calcium nitrate per five gallons nutrient. Between sixth and ninth weeks use six grams calcium phosphate. After that use three grams calcium phosphate.

Yellowing of older leaves around the veins, quickly spreading to the whole plant; veins have varicose appearance=magnesium shortage. Add six grams magnesium sulfate per five gallons nutrient. Magnesium deficiency cannot occur with Formula C because the dosage is intentionally high. In fact during this time you should watch out for magnesium overdose. Symptoms of this are pale green leaves with brown wilting at the edges. If this occurs cut the basic quantity of magnesium salts in half for one week and then bring it gradually up again. This can be easily accomplished by draining half of your tank and then replacing the drained liquids with a special preparation of Formula C which contains no magnesium salts. After that you can continue with regular replacements of normal Formula C preparation.

Yellowing of younger leaves with varicose appearance=iron deficiency. Plant only needs traces, but before adding any iron compounds you should check the acidity of the nutrient solution. The plants will have difficulty absorbing iron if the pH factor exceeds 8. If this is the case add dilute sulfuric acid (3 parts acid, 7 parts water) until pH is normal (pH 5-7). If alkalinity is not the cause of the problem add one ounce of micronutrient concentrate per five gallons nutrient solution. If deficiency symptoms persist after one week dissolve 1/2 gram of iron sulfate in 1/2 cup of water with a few drops of sulfuric acid and add this amount to each five gallons of nutrient solution.

Yellowing of all the leaves; turning brownish orange later; roots appear shorter than normal in their lateral spread and are swollen at their ends=chlorine deficiency. If the prescribed amounts of potassium or magnesium chloride are included in Formulae A, B and C this deficiency cannot possibly occur.

Leaves too small, wrinkled at edges and yellow around veins; not many leaves at bottom and possibly only at top; large gaps between one leaf branch and the next=zinc deficiency. These symptoms are most likely to occur when plant is four to six weeks old. The plants do not absorb this element very well if the pH factor is above 8. Correct pH as described above. Otherwise add one ounce micronutrient per five gallons nutrient.

Swelling and cracking at base of stem exposing dry rotted inside=boron deficiency. **Add** one ounce micronutrient concentrate per five gallons nutrient solution.

Yellowing between the veins of the middle part of the plant, later affecting the top leaves too; new leaves will be twisted=molybdenum shortage. When large amounts of ammonium nitrate are used as in Formula A the yellowing may not occur, but the twisting will. If the pH factor is not at fault add one ounce micronutrient per five gallons nutrient. Without molybdenum the plant cannot properly utilize nitrogen in cell growth.

Whenever any chemicals are added to the nutrient solution test the pH factor. Once every two weeks run a routine test of both acidity and all of the major elements. Soil test kits are available at Sears Roebuck or any nursery and cost about $7. There are many other important things to know about growing supergrass, such as harvesting for maximum resin production and retention. These are discussed in detail in *The Complete Cannabis Cultivator* (see ad on back cover).

EXPLORING THE UNKNOWN

In some parts of Mexico farmers simply stick the marijuana seeds in the soil and depart until harvest time. But they are very cautious that the moon is right for planting. It should, most moon-conscious farmers say, be full and in a water sign (Scorpio, Pisces or Cancer). Experiments in which people prayed over plants indicate that prayer is beneficial to plant growth. Perhaps the plants just appreciate that someone cares enough to pray. Vegetable life seems to be quite sensitive to good and bad vibrations. EEG (electroencephalograph) tests lend support to the green thumb concept. A former police lie detector expert found that when violent and negative feelings were being experienced or when pain was being inflicted upon any animal life, plants in the immediate vicinity showed disturbed patterns on the EEG. Many pot farmers claim that playing music for plants improves them in various ways. Some say that a steady diet of sitar music augments resin production. It is prudent not to get too strung out on any of these claims, but it is also wise not to scoff at them too readily.

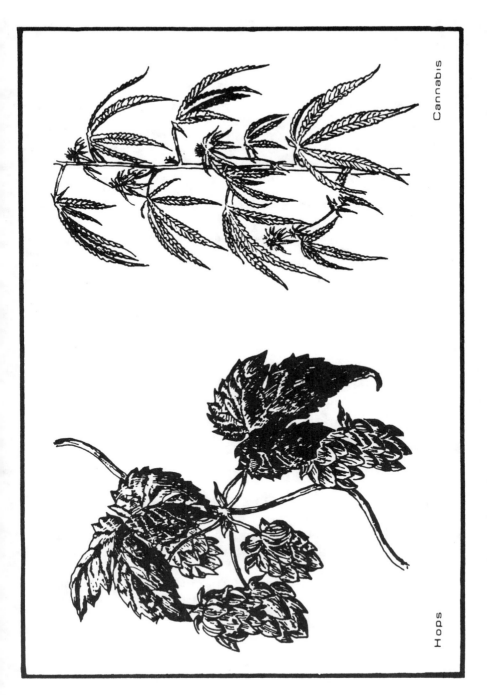

Cannabis

Hops

HOW TO GROW POT PLANTS
THAT DON'T LOOK LIKE MARIJUANA

It is less expensive for the United States to import various kinds of hemp fiber from such distant places as the Philippines than it is to grow her own. During wartime, however, the normal water lanes may be cut off or endangered. For this reason a few American farmers have been given permits to raise cannabis crops for seed. In the event of a large-scale war the nation will always have an abundance of hemp seed ready for planting. These seeds are harvested annually and the rest of the plant is plowed under. After six years storage most cannabis seeds are no longer viable. The outdated supply is sterilized and sold as canary food. The U.S. and several other concerned institutions frequently have sponsored experimental research with hemp growing.

Shortly after America entered World War II, a pair of investigators tried to produce an improved hybrid by grafting cannabis plants onto the rootstocks of hops (*Humulus lupulus*). Hops is the only near relative of marijuana. It even produces a mildly narcotic resin, lupuline, which is chemically akin to THC. Since both plants have similar chemistry as well as being members of the same family, it was reasonable to assume that the graft had a good chance of succeeding. But it failed. However, when the situation was reversed —that is, when hops vines were grafted onto cannabis rootstocks—not only was the transfer successful, but the leaves of the matured hop plants contained as much cannabinol resins as the original marijuana plants would have produced. In other words what you come up with is a thirty-foot-long vegetable which to all observers looks like an ordinary law-abiding hops vine, but which secretly contains all the stoning chemistry of high quality pot. Apparently the resin production of marijuana originates in the roots. Although the government felt that this botanical phenomenon could contribute nothing to the war effort many heads are likely to find value in a "marijuana" plant which can escape the notice of the narcs because it appears to be another plant (see comparative illustration).

HOW TO GRAFT HOPS TO MARIJUANA

Although there are numerous methods of grafting, the ground-level wedge graft is described here because it is the kind used in the original experiments described above and it leaves showing the least possible amount of actual marijuana (about an inch and a half of stem and no foliage).

1.) Construct or procure a large flat bed no less than six inches deep and fill nearly to the top with good soil which has an acidity between pH 5 and 7. Work in some manure, but not too much, and do not use any high nitrogen chemical fertilizers as this will lessen the survival chances of the grafts

or

Use flower pots and follow the same soil and depth requirements described above

or

Use the site on which you plan to grow your pot-hop vines

or

If you with to attempt this project in a hydroponic growing table use a moderate nitrogen formula. HYPONEX is fine. If you mix your own nutrient use a preparation similar to Formula B described in the article on hydroponics in this manual. Do not use Formula A or C at this time or your grafts may perish.

2.) Having chosen one of these growing places, plant seeds from the very best marijuana you can get your hands on. Highest quality Michoacan, Panama Red, Vietnam or Acapulco Gold are preferred. Because of environmental influences any of these are likely to be natural triploid or tetraploid varieties, that is, they may have one or two extra sets of chromosomes. Such mutants not only produce more resin, but are also larger, healthier and more likely to survive grafting.

3.) As the plants grow weed out the inferior ones which tend to crowd the others. By 45 days from the time of planting they should be spaced about ten inches apart, or one to a flower pot.

4.) At the same time that you start the marijuana also plant hop seeds. Choose one of several polyploid varieties available at most seed houses. Follow the same soil and planting instructions as for marijuana.

5.) When the plants are 45 days old lay some kind of marker (a toothpick or matchstick will do) at the base of each marijuana plant parallel to the cotyledons (the unserrated first leaves that came out of the seed). With a single-edge razor blade sever these plants below the cotyledons, about an inch and a half above the ground (Fig. 1). Discard or smoke the upper portion of the plants.

6.) Sever all of the hops plants at approximately the same point. Make sure that at least an inch of stem extends below the cotyledons to the point of severance. Uproot and discard the lower portion of these plants.

7.) Split each marijuana stem about 1/2 inch downward from the point of severance. Make this split perpendicular to the marker which represents the directions in which the cotyledons extended from the stem (Fig. 2).

8.) Cut a slant about 1/2 inch long at the base of each hop stem. Make the cut perpendicular to the cotyledons of the hop scion (Fig. 3).

9.) Insert the hop scion into the split in the marijuana stock so that the slanted wedge-wound of the hop makes direct contact with one side of the split-wound in the marijuana. Allow about 1/16 inch of the hop's slanted wound to show above the severance point of the marijuana stock.

10.) Bind the graft with flat grafting raffia about midway between the top and bottom of the split.

11.) Smear graft sealer around the wound. Graft sealer and binding raffia are available from most nurseries.

12.) Allow the wound dressing to remain on the plants for about ten days. During this time be sure that the plants receive adequate water and are not exposed to the hot sun for long periods. TRANSPLANTONE can be added to the first water to lessen the shock of the graft.

13. After ten days remove the dressing. The surgery should now be satisfactorily healed.

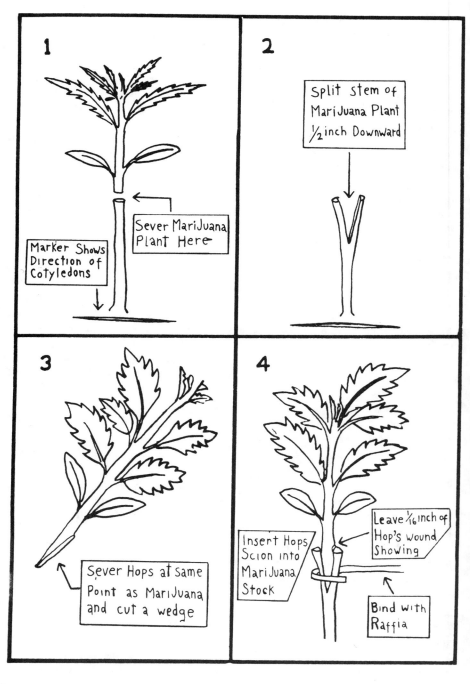

14.) After an additional ten days the "hop" vine may be transplanted to its final growing site. The vines should be planted at least four feet apart and given a fence or preferably an arbor on which to climb. The leaves can be harvested, dried and smoked in the same manner as marijuana.

It is not the author's place to advise whether or not you would be breaking the law by owning cannabinated hop vines. No such case has ever been tested in the courts. It is unlikely that narcotics agents would ever discover your secret and if they did it is very possible that you would eventually win your case. But this could be costly and time-consuming. The hassle of standing trial can in many ways be worse than the penalty. Also bear in mind that it is illegal in the United States to grow the marijuana seedlings required in making this graft.

The hops fruit is used in beermaking as a flavoring. If any readers are interested in home brewing they might try the fruit of "potted" hops for a unique experience in beer drinking. Those who do are warned that beer also contains the toxin alcohol.

PRODUCING SUPERIOR BREEDS OF MARIJUANA

Mention has already been made of marijuana polyploids. These are superior plants which carry extra sets of chromosomes. They are larger, healthier, and richer in resin than normal diploids. Polyploids either occur naturally as a result of environment or can be induced by treatment with colchicine, a toxic substace derived from saffron. To accomplish this dissolve one part colchicine in one hundred parts distilled water and soak the seeds in this solution for twelve hours at 100° F. before planting. Colchicine is toxic to both humans and plants. Handle it with extreme care. Wear rubber gloves, and don't get any in your mouth or eyes. When transferring the seeds to the germinating beds use tweezers, but apply very gentle pressure and grip the seed by its sides rather than its edge. Start at least one hundred seeds in this experiment. A large percentage of the seeds and seedlings will not survive treatment with this powerful substance, but many of those which do will become polyploids. These are clearly recognizable. They have darker, firmer and thicker foliage than the ordinary varieties. Also the flowers, pollen grains and seeds are much larger. These plants will be either triploids (three sets of chromosomes), tetraploids (four sets), or pentaploids (five sets). Of these the tetraploid is usually preferable because it has even sets of chromosomes and therefore reproduces best. There is some evidence, however, that the triploid has a slightly higher resin count than the tetraploid. Get rid of all non-polyploidal plants before maturity so that no diploid males accidentally pollinate any polyploid females. To retain their superior characteristics in future generations polyploids should cross only with other polyploids. Some overly cautious writers have warned against smoking colchicine-treated plants. They suggest that the grower wait until a second generation of plant is produced. This caution may be applicable where the older seedlings or near-mature plants have been exposed to the chemical. The amount which a seed might absorb, however, would be negligible when diffused through an entire plant. Besides this most of the colchicine will have been dissipated after several months of growth. Colchicine is somewhat difficult to obtain. It is sometimes employed as a treatment for gout and is usually sold only by prescription.

STIMULATING GROWTH WITH HORMONES

Another chemical which can be used on plants is the growth stimulant gibberellic acid. It is available under the following commercial names: Gibberellen, Big Grow, G.A., Big Tabs, Gibrel, Brellin, Plant Shoot, and Gib-Sol. It encourages plants to take more moisture into their tissues and become larger with more profuse foliage. This gives the plant more leaf area for photosynthesis and augments both the quantity and quality of the harvest. Use it as the particular brand indicates on the label. Begin application while the plant is in its seedling stage. Its effect wears off after a while so it is necessary to apply regularly every few weeks. The plants should get no less than fourteen hours of light per day. The lower leaves should be pruned as soon as flower stalks appear so that the resin concentration goes to the top. Gibberellic acid treatments may slightly delay maturity and limit flower production. Its use should be terminated at the time of pruning. This discontinuation also aids resin production by lessening the absorption of water into the plant.

A MODERN MIRACLE

Good quality grass can be made even better by mixing it in a coffee can with an equal apparent volume of dry ice. Leave one small pinhole in the can's plastic cover for evaporation of the carbon dioxide gas and put the can in a freezer to delay the melting of the dry ice. After a few days the dry ice will be gone and the grass will be several times stronger than it was before. How this works is still a mystery. It is possible that the combination of carbon dioxide and extreme cold subtly alters the molecular structure of some of the less potent or non-potent isomers in the plant's THC resin complex. For example if one of the isomers $-CH(CH_3)(CH_2)4CH_3$ were converted to $-CH(CH_3)(CH_2)5CH_3$ it would have three and a half times its original potency.

*   *   *   *   *

Both amateur and professional scientists, technologists and agricultural experimenters labor relentlessly to bring you bigger and better highs. As new discoveries are made Stone Kingdom will see that the public is informed of them. But let us not become too dependent on highs which originate outside of ourselves. Remember: the biggest, best and most permanent high comes from within. It takes time, work, knowledge and devotion to acquire and master this dormant native high. But it is worth it! May the Breath of God be ours forever.

$-M.J.S.$

PUBLISHED BY:

FLASH MAIL ORDER
P.O. BOX 14416
PHILA., PA. 19115

© **MOTA WEST 198**

REPRINTED MARCH 19

THE
POT
BOOK

the history, cultivation, preparation
and other useful facts on marijuana

THE POT BOOK

TABLE OF CONTENTS

PUBLISHED BY:

FLASH MAIL ORDER
P.O. BOX 14416
PHILA., PA. 19115

REPRINTED MARCH 1983

HISTORY

The cultivation of <u>Cannabis</u> <u>sativa</u> in the United States dates back to the days previous to the Revolutionary War when the male half of the plant, commonly called hemp, was grown in a large number of states and used in the manufacture of rope. This rope was primarily used for square-rigged ships of the day. Very little significance was then given to the female hemp plant, which is useless in the rope industry but which carries the stimulating resin, <u>Cannabinol.</u> In later years, when the need for domestic rope declined, so did the cultivation of hemp. Growers of the plant became the exception and after federal legislation they were required to have the authorization of the Government.

Along about 1860 an American anonymously published a book entitled <u>THE HASHISH EATER.</u> The book attached a religious meaning to the effects rendered by the use of <u>Cannabis</u> <u>sativa</u> as a stimulant. Somewhere between this time and the early 20th century marihuana slowly began to become popular in the United States as a stimulant. The origin of this popularity may be traced to two different sources. Many French literary writers such as Dumas and Baudelaire, to mention but a few, aroused keen interest in the use of marihuana when they quite candidly extolled the stimulating effects brought about by this strange herb. It is interesting that these writings, rich with sensuous connotations regarding the plant, brought about the first popular interest in marihuana as a stimulant in Western Europe.

Very early in the 20th century, about 1910, Mexican laborers brought the plant across the border to the United States in large quantities, and eventually it became well established in New Orleans. This city became the center point from where it gradually became popular throughout

1

the rest of the country and parts of Canada. Upon the abolition of alcohol, marihuana gained an added boost, giving it a well established following.

To date very little research has been done on the subject of marihuana smoking. And thus still very little is known about the plant. The most detailed investigation into the effects of Cannabis sativa in the United States took place in the 1930's under the direction of New York's Mayor La Guardia. At that time the investigation revealed that marihuana was sold mainly in cigarette form. The cost ranged from seventeen cents each to as high as one dollar per cigarette. The latter was said to consist of African hemp or "gungeon", which apparently was a stronger concentration of the intoxicating resin. The report stated that in the Harlem area of New York City there were at that time several hundred places where marihuana was sold, and it was also reported that the average person using the plant would smoke from eight to ten cigarettes per day. Most of its users, the report notes, were Negro or Latin American. Only a negligible amount was found to be used by school aged children. Later, in the 1940's, a report by Bromberg and Rodgers stated that no relation between crime and the use of marihuana could be found.

Cannabis sativa was called "hashish" by the Persians. It later became known as "marijuana" in the United States, a word which is believed to be Latin American in origin. "Pot" and "grass" are American innovations for the same substance. There have been countless other nicknames for marihuana, some of them rather sick sounding, such as "joy weed", which was popular during the La Guardia investigation. Today "pot" and "grass" are most popular, although the expression "smoke some dope" also refers to marihuana. The term "hashish" now refers to a far more refined version of marihuana and it bears a far greater concentration of the resin Cannabinol.

2

THE ISSUE

Marihuana as an issue has never been fully brought before the public's eye. At least not until very recent times. It has heretofore been allowed to carry the same fearful connotations as those brought about by the mention of heroin and other opiates. In actuality, the link between the two is due more to American journalists, eager for a headline, than the less interesting research done by a few serious scientists and sociologists. It is only recently that a more serious consideration has been given to marihuana. And this has been offered by a select few who have been courageous enough to publically advocate its legalization. Many have been immediately shunned, like the school teacher in California who was immediately dismissed when she announced that she had been smoking pot for years. Others, finding this road too difficult, have denounced the stiff laws regulating marihuana and also the ignorance which has made even mention of the word a social "taboo". It has, however, at long last become a serious issue in the 1960's and most probably will prevail as such until it is either legalized or successfully kept beyond the borders of the United States.

The legalization of marihuana in the United States is an issue which must eventaully fall upon the wisdom of our legislators and courts. The latter can only offer aid or hindrance by either following the present laws to the letter or by interpreting them more in light of present times. The legislators, however, must respond in the interest of society as a whole, which most unfortunately will eventually include a strong lobby backed by the liquor industry. A not-so-unrelated example of powerful lobbies is the secret war between the railroad industry and the trucking lines. When trucking companies first posed a serious threat to the railroad, prompt legislation was inacted which, in many states, placed undue handicaps on truckers. Some railroads even went so far as to convince the public that trucks on the highways meant a serious threat to our safety. They scandalized remote incidents in which a truck had collided with another automobile. The powerful lobby of the gun industry is still another example of the pressures placed on our legislators.

But just as people kill with guns and trucks are a far more superior method of shipping, people smoke pot. All the kings horses were unable to prevent the inevitable decline of the railroad. And it seems that all the kings men are only going to make pot even more popular than it already is.

Above all marihuana has been accused of being the "precursor" of the opiates. The legislator who casts his vote "for" the legalization of marihuana must always wonder about this accusation. Should it be true, marihuana must be abolished without a doubt. It has been safely attested, however, that marihuana is not habit forming. Upon the cessation of its use there are no withdrawal symptoms as in both alcoholics and addicts of heroin. People do not crave marihuana as they might alcohol, cigarettes and drugs. Extensive use of marihuana is said to create symptoms of dulling the senses, especially the thought process. The steady user may also feel a slight or vague state of fatigue, possibly with muscular aches and pains. These symptoms disappear immediately upon the cessation of its use.

It can be safely assumed that most all of the various questions about pot can and will eventually be answered to everyone's satisfaction (or dissatisfaction). The argument that pot leads to the use of heroin is invalid in many people's minds, especially those who smoke pot and have no desire to try heroin. Some argue that although many heroin addicts claim to have first tried pot, they must also have tried coffee, cigarettes and that dread intoxicant, alcohol. And according to more recent reports there are fourteen times as many marihuana users than there are heroin users. It also appears that heroin users never return to marihuana. It has thus been condluded by one investigator that "most marihuana users do not become heroin users." (DRUG ADDICTION IN YOUTH by Ernest Harms).

And it stands to reason. The occasional beer drinker is not generally considered to be on his way to alcoholism. Whiskey is not a logical step from beer. And even on occasions when it is the lure of addiction comes more from within than from the intoxicant.

WHY LEGALIZE POT ?

The reasons for legalizing marihuana are manifold, some of them stemming from the firm belief that the laws presently against marihuana are a hoax. Another reason lies in the way marihuana is presently imported into the United States and further, how it is prepared before it crosses these borders.

Pot, or, as the Mexicans call it, "mota", is grown in great abundance in the central regions of Mexico. And it is from there that the largest amount of the plant finds its way into the United States. The Mexicans prepare a kilo (2.2 pounds) of marihuana by first cutting the plant about the mid-stem and hanging it upside down so that it both dries and also so that any of the resin left in the stem will flow into the leaves. After this process is concluded the semi-dry plant is crumbled partially and laid out, where it is seasoned with rum. The harvestor will sip a quantity of rum and then spray it through his lips onto the newly harvested plant. This process finished, a kilo is measured

5

out and the plant is then compressed into a brick-like cube weighing exactly 2.2 pounds. The rum gives the plant a special substance and taste. Occasionally it is replaced by opium. There are probably still other methods of preparation. The ultimate consumer never knows.

The danger is, then, very high to the ultimate consumer. He has absolutely no way of knowing what he has purchased. Thus the conditions under which a normal product is presented to the general public ·for sale are ignored, since there is no jurisdiction by the Food and Drugs Administration nor, for that matter, the Federal Trade Commission. This aspect is slight at the present, but will become increasingly important if the use of marihuana continues to rise, as it seems to be doing.

WHAT IS IT LIKE TO BE HIGH ON POT

Some of the more serious aspects of this forbidden herb having been discussed, let's turn to what people really see in smoking pot. A normal high on pot will usually last anywhere from two to six hours, depending upon both the person and the quantity he has smoked or ingested. There is no such thing as "overindulgence" since each individual instinctively knows when he or she has had enough. The word might more properly refer to the frequency of its use rather than the quantity.

The first sensation is that of lightheadedness and in some individuals exhilaration. Hunger and sleepiness are often very prevalent sensations. One may daydream. Inhibitions decrease. A sombre stage of relaxation is quickly reached and one's senses become incredibly acute, or so it appears to the user. Music is popular with pot smokers for this reason. The most crude piece of music often seems to

6

resound like a full orchestra. It flows about a room like a heavy tide, all engulfing. Hallucinations occasionally occur, but these are usually prompted by the user himself and are under one's control at all times. Time seems exaggerated tremendously, so that a mere few seconds may seem like a long while. Speech comes easy and one is delighted with one's own cleverness of speech and improvisations. The most common of thoughts or occurances appear as revelations. Memory is short. Concentration is difficult. It is relatively easy to laugh and giggle. The novice smoker of pot will do this incessantly while the more experienced user becomes accustomed to this light feeling and is able to channel it to other sensations. Although marihuana is not an aphrodisiac, sexual experiences seem much greater since the passage of time seems so much longer, thus making the experience more impressive. Food is most delightful also because the senses have become more acute. Apetite is often endless. The most dull foods become delicious. One's outward appearance changes only in that the user's eyes may become bloodshot and he will laugh where there is no apparent humor. Pot smokers customarily enjoy being with each other 'to get high, although good conversation is rare during such sessions.

MARIHUANA VS ALCHOHOL

To one accustomed to a high on alcohol, marihuana is more pleasant since there are no after effects aside from a vague feeling of fatigue and tiredness. Frequent use, though, will cause this feeling to become chronic. Marihuana does not cause headaches or digestion problems. It is non-habit forming and, as stated before, will lead to the use of heroin about as often as alcohol will lead to alcoholism. Marihuana can be said to be psychologically habit forming, but there is never a physical "craving" for the herb.

Alcohol is ingested directly into the stomach, endangering the liver in many cases where the user overindulges too frequently. Both introduce the individual into a non-real world. Alcohol is considered to be a depressant, marihuana a stimulant. The former dulls the senses, the latter confuses them.

The user of marihuana becomes restful and introspective. A high on alcohol will cause the user to often overestimate his abilities and often perform irrational acts. A high on marihuana causes absent-mindedness. The powers of concentration are immensely decreased with marihuana.

HOW MARIHUANA IS PREPARED

The preparation of marihuana as a stimulant is achieved by harvesting the leaves and sprouts of the female hemp plant Cannabis sativa, and the most important procedure is the curing of this plant. But first it is important to be able to identify the female plant, since it is undesirable to include the male plant. This male plant is merely hemp and does not contain the resin Cannabinol. The female plant is actually unmistakable since it has many more flowers than the male plant. These flowers are a yellow-green color. The leaves are usually three to six inches in length and are darker in color on the top. The edges of the leaves are saw-like in appearance and have rather definite ridges running from the center to its outer borders. See page 15 and look closely at the illustration.

8

HOW TO GROW YOUR OWN POT

Since in the United States it is illegal at present to grow Cannabis sativa, it is not recommended that the reader experiment with his own. The first step would logically be to collect the seeds. From the seeds one must select the darker of the lot and set them aside, for they will break through their shells more easily. Green seeds very rarely will sprout since the plant will be unable to break through the tough shell of the seed. These darker seeds should be planted first in a wooden box, about 3/4 of an inch below the surface. The earth on top of the seeds should not be packed hard, but left loose. Usually the first plant or plants will sprout up within a few days, although others will take up to a week to ten days. Well fertilized soil, of course, enhances the plants chances of survival. Since pot grows best in tropical and temperate climates, North Americans should have little difficulties with the climate. It should be mentioned that hemp has been successfully grown in every state on the continent, and presently grows wild in many of them.

Once the plant has reached about two inches high, it should be transplanted to a regular flower pot where it may easily be watered from the bottom. Although marihuana needs plenty of water and sunshine, over watering, especially from the top, will cause the plant to rot at the base of its stem. Eventually it will tumble sideways and die. Thus never allow the uppermost part of the soil to become wet. Water the plant from the bottom every few days, depending upon the weather. Give it plenty of sunshine but bring it indoors at nighttime if the weather is too chilly.

Once the plant has reached high enough where a good harvest may be had, one must separate or distinguish the male from the female plant. The plant should be cut about mid-stem since the bottom half will then quickly continue to grow once again. These leaves may be dried quickly in an oven, but it is a crude way of curing the herb. The longer process has already been described and it is highly recommendable to employ this method. Again, depending upon the climate, about four weeks should be enough to allow the leaves to dry. Hanging the plant upside down will greatly enhance the stimulating effects. A little rum or wine might be sprayed over the harvest to give it a tobacco like quality in the sense that it will have more substance. Entirely dry leaves will naturally pulverize and make a poor smoke which will draw with much difficulty.

It is also important that the seeds and stalks be separated from the leaves and sprouts, and that none of the male leaves are used by mistake. At best these will cause a harsh smoke and the seeds are said to cause a headache.

HOW POT IS SOLD

A kilo is usually born somewhere in the interior regions of Mexico, where it is cured and prepared into a brick-like form which weighs 2.2 pounds or one kilo. This kilo is sold for about $30.00 to $50.00. Once it crosses the border it will be worth $80.00 to $120.00 in California and the further from the border the higher the price. For instance, $150.00 in Seattle. In the East the prices are often astronomical. A "lid" is one ounce and it will sell for about $10.00. Street vendors package these lids and in this form such an individual may profit over $300.00 per kilo. The risk of street vending is much greater since the seller must expose himself to strangers to sell his goods. It should be noted that a drug addict may make a purchase once a day. Since marihuana is relatively inexpensive, the user may make a purchase once every two

10

months. This lack of exposure between buyer and seller decreases the ability of the police in making arrests.

Marihuana is also grown in California in the valley regions. This is done by amateurs and its cultivation is far inferior to that of the Mexicans.

ROLLING JOINTS

This pertains to one's personal preference. Nothing beats a good hand rolled joint, but the art seems to be on the wane. Small hand gadgets are becoming more and more popular to roll joints. They cost about one dollar and will last a long while. They are easy to use and normally good directions come with each one. Cigarette paper is also of personal preference. Licorice paper is quite popular because it gives the smoke a sweet, smooth taste. Non-smokers should try this type first. It should be the least harsh. Most all papers will function as well, however. More recently flavored paper has been introduced, and these come in a variety of flavors, including chocolate and strawberry. A paper should not burn too quickly, if at all, since it causes too much waste.

WATER PIPES

Some smokers swear by water pipes, which now come in a variety of styles. A fine water pipe may be made from an empty wine bottle which is fat enough at the bottom to give it ballast and narrow at the neck. It should merely be corked with two small pipes running through the cork. Attached to one is a container for the ashes. This runs down into the water. Attached to the other is a hose from which the pipe is smoked. Wine is often used instead of water, which is said to give the smoke a special taste.

TEA AND COOKIES

Tea is self-explanatory. Unfortunately, great quantities must be ingested to attain a high from this method. Cookies are always popular as an extra. Any recipe may be used. There are no "special" recipes. Just add a sufficient amount of pot. They should be eaten on an empty stomach to be sure that enough of the resin is absorbed into the system.

WON'T YOU HAVE TEA WITH ME?

2 tablespoons seeds	honey
2 tea bags	oranges
1 tablespoon pot	cinnamon stick

Boil 4 cups water with seeds and pot for 15 minutes, add tea bags and honey to taste, serve in cups containing large chunks of oranges and cinnnamon stick.

HOT POT FUDGE

1/2 cup pot
2 packages (2 cups) semisweet chocolate pieces   1 teaspoon vanilla
3/4 cup sweetened condensed milk   1/2 cup pot

Melt semisweet chocolate over hot (not boiling) water. Remove from heat; stir in milk, vanilla, pot. Mix well. Turn into buttered pan or shape as desired. Let stand several hours or overnight.
Makes about 1-1/4 lbs.

SPAGHETTI SAUCE

1 can (six oz.) tomato paste	1 bay leaf
1 can (six oz.) water	1/2 cup chopped pot
2 tablespoons olive oil	1 pinch thyme
1/2 clove minced garlic	1 pinch pepper
1/2 cup chopped onion	1/2 teaspoon salt

Mix in a pot, cover and simmer with frequent stirring for thirty minutes. Serve over spaghetti.

CHILI POT

2 lbs. pinto beans
1/2 clove garlic
1 lb. bacon, cut in 2 inch sections
1 cup pot

2 cups red wine
1/2 cup mushrooms
4 tablespoons chili powder

Soak beans overnight. In a large pot pour boiling water over beans and simmer for at least an hour, adding more water to keep beans covered. Now add all other ingredients and continue to simmer for another three hours. Salt to taste.
Serves ten.

THE MEAT BALL

1 lb. hamburger
1/4 cup bread crumbs
1/4 cup chopped onions

3 tablespoons chopped pot
1 can cream of mushroom soup
3 tablespoons india relish

Mix it all up and shape into meat balls. Brown in a frying pan and drain. Place in a casserole with soup and 1/2 can of water, cover and cook over low heat for about 30 minutes.
Serves four.

POT BROWNIES

1/2 cup pot
1/2 cup flour
1/4 teaspoon baking powder
3 tablespoons shortening
1/2 cup sugar
2 tablespoons honey

2 tablespoons corn syrup
1 egg (beaten)
1 square melted chocolate
1 tablespoon vanilla
1/2 cup chopped nuts
pinch salt

Sift flour, baking powder and salt together. Mix shortening, sugar, honey, syrup and egg. Blend in chocolate then the other ingredients, mix well. Spread in an 8" pan and bake for 20 minutes at 350°

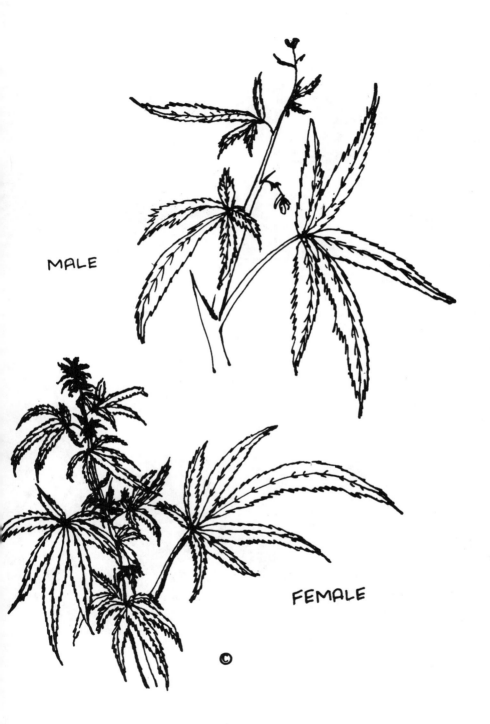

MALE

FEMALE

©

14

Come on, Arnie, quit smoking it all, or there won't be enough left to make the goddamn cookies!"

"Hey, how about that, Sarge, he _is_ with the narcotics detail!"

15

THE MARIJUANA CONSUMER'S AND DEALER'S GUIDE

with the new superior mescaline process

endorsed by the grass prophet

mary jane superweed

$1.50

Produced by STONE KINGDOM SYNDICATE

TABLE OF CONTENTS

Cover by Michelangelo Buonarroti and Friends

The author, editor and publisher of this book assume no responsibility for failures and damages resulting from the use of the substances or processes herein described. Nor do they encourage the use of these substances and processes in countries or states where they are forbidden by law. This book is printed for its educational value and as a humble addition to the total of mankind's knowledge.

1983

𝕾tone 𝕶ingdom 𝕾yndicate

All Rights Reserved

PUBLISHED BY:

FLASH MAIL ORDER
P.O. BOX 14416
PHILA., PA. 19115

TO EXTRACT LYSERGIC ACID AMIDES FROM MORNING GLORY OR HAWAIIAN WOOD ROSE SEEDS

1.) In an osterizer, pepper grinder or coffee grinder grind 100 grams of Heavenly Blue morning glory seeds or baby Hawaiian wood rose seeds.

2.) Soak for 2 days in 120 cc of petroleum ether (industrial quality petroleum ether is suitable).

3.) Filter solution through a paper filter.

4.) Discard liquid.

5.) Allow mash to dry completely.

6.) Soak dried mash for 2 days in 100 cc. of methyl (wood) alcohol.

7.) Filter solution.

8.) Save liquid and label "Solution A."

9.) Resoak mash for 2 days in 100 cc. methyl alcohol.

10.) Filter.

11.) Discard mash.

12.) Add liquid to solution A.

13.) Pour solution into a large, flat tray and let evaporate outside or in a well-ventilated room. Do not use flame (methyl alcohol is inflammable). Guard from direct sunlight as this may reduce potency.

14.) When alcohol is gone a yellow gum remains. This may be scraped up, rolled with just enough flour to remove tackiness and stuffed into capsules. Any gum that remains stuck to tray may be dissolved with water and drunk.

The yield is 1 strong dose per 30 grams of morning glory seeds or per 15 seeds of Hawaiian wood rose.

NOTE OF CAUTION:

In the United States morning glory seeds are often coated with a toxic chemical so that instead of becoming expanded consciously you will become poisoned physically. For this reason do not use Northrop-King seeds. If toxin is used it will be mentioned on the package or sack. Soaking the seeds in warm water for 20 minutes removes most of the toxins. This must be done before the seeds have been ground or crushed or most of the amides will also be removed.

It is more economical to purchase morning glory seeds in bulk from a large seed supply house rather than in small packages.

Baby Hawaiian wood rose is found on most floral stands or may be ordered from:

> Magic Garden Herb Company
> P.O. Box 332
> Fairfax, Calif 94930

For further information about morning glory, Hawaiian wood rose and many other natural and legal highs send for *Herbal Highs* (see ad on back cover).

TO PRODUCE HASHISH FROM MARIJUANA

1.) Break up kilo of marijuana and sift through a screen.

2.) Place sifted leaf in a large pot.

3.) Separate seeds from stems by shaking seeds down an inclined newspaper. (Seeds are not used because they contain much oil which makes the final product messy. But save seeds for planting or for Superweed recipe on page 11.)

4.) Add stems to leaf. (They may be pulverized through an osterizer first.)

5.) Cover leaf and stems with isopropyl (rubbing) alcohol, about 1½ gallons per kilo. (Rubbing alcohol may be had for the lowest price in cut-rate drug stores such as Walgreen's or Merrill's or at some supermarkets such as Mayfair [about 19 cents per pint]. If processing a large quantity it is better to order industrial quality isopropyl alcohol from a chemical company.

6.) Place lid on pot and boil for 3 hours on electric hot plate. (Caution: alcohol is inflammable; do not cook on gas flame.)

7.) Strain liquids and store in container labeled "Solution A."

8.) Repeat steps 5 through 7 using fresh alcohol.

9.) After two alcohol extractions repeat steps 5 and 6 twice, using water instead and boiling at higher temperature than with alcohol. Boil each time for 1 hour.

10.) Strain these liquids and store in container labeled "Solution B."

11.) Reduce volume of solution A by boiling in a large pot. (Work outside or in well-ventilated room.)

12.) Reduce volume of solution B by boiling in a separate pot. (Gas flame is safe with solution B.)

13.) When both solutions are considerably reduced (but not too thick), combine the two solutions and boil down further on hot plate. Lower temperature as mixture thickens.

14.) Sprinkle 1½ oz. pulverized pine resin, a little at a time, in fine layers onto the surface of the extract while stirring it in thoroughly. Do not dump in too much at a time or it will form clumps. The purpose of the resin is to act as a binder. Without it the hash may have a tendency to become soft and gooey after a few days. This soft condition will not negate the smokability of the substance, but it will be very much like opium, which melts and bubbles while burning. Pine resin may be ordered from Magic Garden Herb Co., P.O. Box 332, Fairfax, Calif. 94930 $2 per 1½ oz.

15.) After resin is thoroughly stirred in, continue to boil the extract down to the consistency of heavy grease. (*Caution:* When hot this substance is in a molten state and appears as a liquid. In this state there is danger of burning or reducing potency if cooked too long or at too high a temperature.

16.) When this substance is about the thickness of heavy grease pour it about one-half inch thick into a teflon baking tin which is at least 2 inches deep.

17.) Heat oven to 350° for 15 minutes. Turn off. Place tin in upper oven for 15 minutes.

18.) Remove tin and allow to cool.

19.) If cool hashish is still tacky repeat steps **19** and **20** until hard hashish is produced.

20.) When hard, if you wish to divide hashish into ounces or grams, warm for 10 minutes in low temperature oven, remove and cut immediately with table knife.

One kilo of marijuana yields about seven ounces of hashish. At the current hash price of $85 per ounce this is worth $595; it may be divided into 200 grams, which at current rates of $8 to $10 per gram is worth $1600 to $2000.

At the time of the first printing of *The Marijuana Consumer's and Dealer's Guide* the price of marijuana was much lower than it is today. (You may thank Nixon for this.) At the current price it may not appear economically worthwhile to convert grass to hash, especially since the price of hashish has not increased in proportion to that of pot. However, many people are growing their own grass and turning it into hash. This, although illegal, can be even more economically rewarding than using grass bought at the pre-Nixon price. For information on growing marijuana read *The Complete Cannabis Cultivator* and *The Super Grass Grower's Guide* (see ad on back cover of this book).

—M.J.S.

HOW NOT TO GET BURNED

When purchasing large quantities of LSD, mescaline, psilocybin, etc., always follow these simple rules:

1. Do your dealing straight over the table. Do not front your money.

2. If holding a large amount of money do not go alone with people you do not know and trust. If the deal looks shady. do *not* bring a gun or weapon to protect yourself as this may lead to violence, injury and legal trouble. *When in doubt don't deal.* Most trouble ensues from *greed* and *impatience.* These are two "deadly sins" which deserve no place in the psychedelic culture.

3. Always select one random tablet or capsule from the batch you are going to purchase. Do not accept any food or beverage from the seller. It sometimes happens that real LSD is slipped into a cup of coffee while all of the capsules are duds.

TO EXTRACT PURE MESCALINE FROM PEYOTE
New Improved Method

1.) Boil 1 kilo of dried peyote buttons in a large pressure cooker with enough water to cover buttons (about 3 quarts).

2.) Save the liquid and repeat the process until the buttons no longer have a bitter taste. This takes about five boilings.

3.) Strain the extracted liquids to remove pulp particles. Then boil the combined liquids down to a concentrate about the thickness of cream. This should be about 800 ml.

4.) Add 400 grams of sodium hydroxide (lye). Stir until thoroughly dissolved. The lye renders the mescaline more soluble in benzene and less soluble in water. If all of these instructions are properly followed no lye will go into the mescaline-benzene solution.

5.) If you have a large separatory funnel (see Illustration A) pour this mixture into it, add 1600 ml. of benzene, shake gently but thoroughly for about five minutes and let stand for two hours. If you don't have a separatory funnel use a one-gallon jug with siphon (see Illustration B).

6.) After standing for two hours the benzene layer will separate and go to the top while the water layer stays on the bottom. After this happens drain off water layer and save in a jug labeled "tea." Put benzene into a jug labeled "benzene layer." If separation has been done in a jug instead of a sep funnel carefully siphon off the benzene layer and save it in the labeled jug. Make certain that none of the water layer goes into the benzene portion. Do not even allow the emulsion layer (the middle layer between the benzene and the water) to go into the benzene. If any of these por-

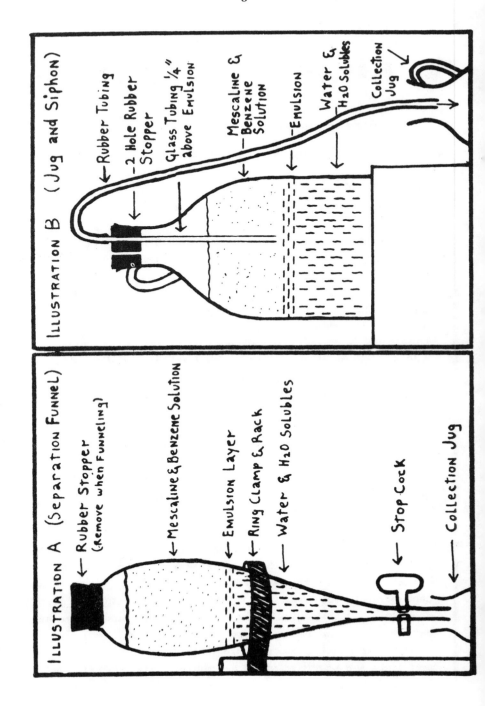

ILLUSTRATION B (Jug and Siphon)

Rubber Tubing

2 Hole Rubber Stopper

Glass Tubing ¼" above Emulsion

Mescaline & Benzene Solution

Emulsion

Water & H₂O Solubles

Collection Jug

ILLUSTRATION A (Separation Funnel)

Rubber Stopper (Remove when Funneling)

Mescaline & Benzene Solution

Emulsion Layer

Ring Clamp & Rack

Water & H₂O Solubles

Stop·Cock

Collection Jug

tions should get into the benzene pour the benzene and water solutions back together and repeat the separation process (steps **5** and **6**). It is better to leave a little of the benzene solution in the "tea" than to risk getting the "tea" or emulsion into the benzene portion. Do not fear that any of the mescaline (in the benzene solution) will be wasted. All will be salvaged later. If the water and benzene layers should fail to separate properly immerse the separatory funnel or jug in hot water. This will help break the emulsion.

7.) Prepare a solution of two parts sulphuric acid in one part water. When mixing add the sulphuric acid to the water, letting it run down the side of the graduate or measuring beaker containing the water. *Caution:* Never pour water into sulphuric acid because it will splatter and do damage.

8.) (**a**) Add 25 drops of this acid solution to the benzene solution, one drop at a time. Put stopper on jug, shake well for a minute and let stand for 5 minutes. Streaks of white mescaline sulphate crystals should begin to form in the benzene bottle. (**b**) Add 25 more drops of acid, shake and wait for 10 minutes. (**c**) Add 15 drops, shake, wait 10 minutes. (**d**) Add 15 drops, shake, wait 15 minutes. (**e**) Add 10 drops, shake, wait 30 minutes. This solution should now be tested with wide range pH paper and should be between pH 7.5 and 8.

9.) Allow precipitate to settle. Then pour benzene off the top into the separation funnel or jug. Be careful not to pour off any of the precipitate.

10.) To the benzene add solution labeled "tea." Shake well for 5 minutes and let stand for 2 hours as in step **5**.

11.) Repeat steps **6-10**. Again save the "tea" as well as the benzene.

12.) Repeat steps **6-10** at least one more time or until no more precipitate is formed. This might mean a total of four times. Use less than half the number of acid drops that was originally used. The final time take only to step **9** and be especially careful and exacting.

13a.) Put the precipitate and residual benzene in a beaker and set beaker in hot water bath (see Illustration C). This will drive off the remaining benzene and dry the crystals.

OR

13b.) An alternative way to accomplish the same result as in **13a** is to pour the precipitate and residual benzene into a Buchner funnel with filter paper (see Illustration D) and, after the benzene has gone through the paper, rinse the benzene solution bottle with 100 ml. of ether and pour it over crystals in filter. After ether has gone through, rinse crystals one more time with 100 ml. ether, then allow them to dry. This process (**13b**) is a little faster than **13a,** but requires that you have ether. Take your choice.

14.) Dissolve crystals in 200 ml. of near-boiling water. Add a pinch of Norit (activated charcoal) and filter while hot through #2 paper. This time save the filtered solution and discard the filter paper. The Norit helps to remove impurities from the crystals. Since the crystals are dissolved in hot water, this time they will pass through the filter paper.

15.) Add 10% ammonia solution to this solution—a few drops at a time until solution is adjusted to pH 6.5-7.

16.) Add a boiling stone and boil solution down to 75 ml. Then allow to cool.

17.) Place solution in freezer or in refrigerator turned to coldest temperature and allow to cool to near freezing. Long, white, needle-like crystals will form.

18.) Immediately (while solution is still near freezing) break crystal matrix and filter. The mescaline sulphate crystals are insoluble in water when close to freezing so they will not go through the filter

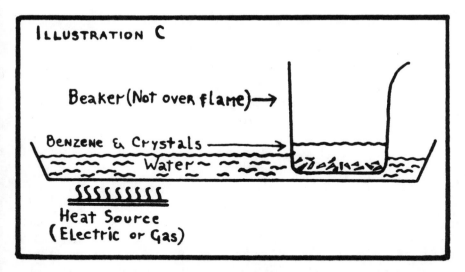

ILLUSTRATION C

Beaker(Not over flame)→

Benzene & Crystals ————→

~~Water~~

Heat Source
(Electric or Gas)

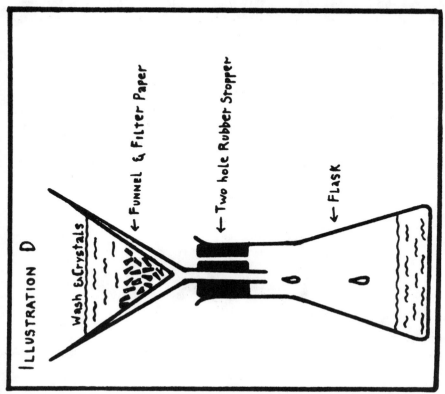

ILLUSTRATION D

Wash & Crystals

← Funnel & Filter Paper

← Two hole Rubber Stopper

← Flask

this time.

19.) After filtering crystals pour a little ice water over them and filter again.

20.) Crystals should be pure white now. Dry them on a plate in a low temperature oven, under a heat lamp or in some warm place. Do not let temperature exceed 120° C.

Yield: 18 to 20 grams or 36 to 40 doses at one-half gram per dose.

Save the filtrate (solution that went through the filter paper) from Steps **18** and **19**. Boil down to 20 ml. Refrigerate to crystallize. Filter while cold. If this second crop of crystals appears dirty dissolve in 20 ml. near-boiling water, add a tiny pinch of Norit and filter hot through #2 paper as in step **14**. Refrigerate filtrate and filter cold as in step **18**. These steps should salvage an additional 2 grams of mescaline sulphate (4 doses). Mescaline is strongest in its sulphate form.

The effects of peyote differ in several ways from those of pure mescaline. This is due to the presence of other alkaloids in peyote. Some people prefer one trip, some prefer the other. If you are interested in extracting all of the psychoactive substances from peyote, watch for *Psychedelic Extractions* by Mary Jane Superweed. It will be available very soon.

TO CONVERT INFERIOR GRADE POT
INTO CONNOISSEUR-QUALITY SUPER-GRASS

1.) Sift leaf through a screen.

2.) Place seeds and stems in a large pot and cover with isopropyl (rubbing) alcohol. (If you have saved seeds and stems from other lids and kilos or seeds left over from hashish formula given in this book, these should also be added.)

3.) Cover pot with lid and heat on electric hot plate for 3 hours. (*Caution:* alcohol is inflammable. Do not use gas flame.)

4.) Strain liquids and store in container labeled "Solution A."

5.) Repeat steps **3** and **4** with fresh alcohol.

6.) Repeat steps **3** and **4** with water instead of alcohol. Store in container labeled "Solution B." (This time gas flame may be used with 1 hour boiling time.)

7.) Repeat step **6**.

8.) On an electric hot plate outside or in a well-ventilated room reduce volume of solution A by boiling.

9.) On a gas flame reduce volume of solution B by boiling.

10.) When both solutions are considerably reduced (but not too thick) combine the two solutions and boil down further on hot plate. Lower temperature as mixture thickens.

11.) When this combination begins to get syrupy allow to cool. When cooled it should be about the consistency of a thin syrup. If it is still very watery it may be boiled down further and cooled again.

12.) Place sifted marijuana leaf into same pot with the extracted syrup. Knead it and roll it around in this until leaf is thoroughly and evenly coated with the stuff.

13.) Spread leaf on aluminum foil or baking tin to dry. Do not dry on newspapers as these will absorb the juices. To fast dry: (**a**) pre-heat oven at 300° for 15 minutes, (**b**) turn off heat. (**c**) place baking tin in oven for 15 minutes, (**d**) repeat process until dry.

One kilo of low-grade marijuana makes about 1¼ pounds of clean (seedless, twigless) superweed. Many experts have mistaken it for a high quality import from India or North Africa. It is usually packaged as ½-ounce lids which sell for $10 or $15 each. 1¼ pounds makes 40 lids—$400 to $600 value.

Inferior marijuana can also be somewhat improved by spreading the leaf upon a newspaper and exposing to a sunlamp for 24 hours at a distance of two feet.

THC

Tetrahydrocannabinol (THC) which has been produced synthetically is still (at the time of this printing) legal. However, a federal law will soon be in effect which will add it to the list of illicit substances. The process for making THC is very difficult so it is wise to be doubtful of much of the stuff that is being passed off as THC on the black market.

Some greedy and unethical persons are mixing amphetamines with barbiturates, heavy tranquilizers and belladonna and passing this off on the public as THC. Either of two tests may be used to determine if a substance is really THC: (1) Smoke a tiny portion of the powder. If it is THC it will get you high just like hashish. (2) Dissolve one-fourth of a capsule of the sample in 1 ml. of petroleum ether. In another graduate prepare a solution of 1 part hydrochloric acid and 6 parts absolute alcohol. To 1 ml. of sample solution add 2 ml. of acid-alcohol solution. Shake vigorously in a test tube. Let test tube stand for a minute while the two immiscible liquids separate. If the substance is THC a reddish color will appear at the junction between the two liquids. The upper liquid will be clear and the lower liquid will be a light orange-pink. This lower tint will disappear when you add 1 ml. of water.

While the second of these tests is more complicated it is also more accurate and is the official test for chemical identification of cannabis.

MARIJUANA

Marijuana is sometimes sprayed with lightly sugared water to facilitate compression of the kilos into bricks. If the kilo is too heavily sugared the grass will be sticky, difficult to light and harsh on the throat and lungs. Do not accept heavily sugared grass. If you should get stuck with some it is better not to attempt to wash the sugar out of it if this can be avoided, because much of the potent pollen grains and exuded resins will be lost. If the grass is not too thick with sugar pre-heat an oven to 300°, spread the grass less than an inch deep on a baking tin, place in oven and immediately off heat. Leave tray in oven for 15 minutes. Repeat this process as necessary until grass is no longer sticky. If the marijuana is so badly sugared that washing is necessary, do so in a large container and save the water to be used as tea. Dry the wet grass as described above. Sugared grass can be used in baking marijuana brownies. It may even be wise to purchase sugared grass at a bargain price if you are planning to do some enlightened baking. If you seek a long-lasting high eat 1/6 to 1/3 of an ounce of grass. It takes about an hour to come on but you stay superstoned for three or four hours with a slow, peaceful descent over the next eight to ten hours.

Never front your money to a connection. It is risky and unnecessary. He is making his profit; let him operate with his own capital. If you front money to him and he gets busted after procuring the grass you must sustain the loss. There is no ethical premise by which you could demand repayment.

BEWARE

Some unscrupulous types posing as legitimate and honest dealers will take your money, then tell you that they were stopped by the police and: (a) had to ditch the grass, (b) the cop took the grass, but didn't bust them, (c) they were busted, but the case was dropped on grounds of illegal search and seizure (police do not return illegally seized marijuana to its rightful owner.)

Another way that people frequently get taken is the double door trick. Your connection leaves you to wait outside while he goes into a building to purchase the commodity (with your money). Your friend goes out the back exit. And you stand there waiting.

Be safe. Buy only from a reputable dealer. Fortunately, I have found most dealers honest and dependable. But there are always those few who are lacking in moral fibre.

Do not attempt to smuggle marijuana into the USA from Mexico. It is tempting because the price is so low. But it is foolish. Border customs searches are often very thorough. Federal penalties are severe and for a small amount it's not worth the risk. The Mexican Federal Police usually know where the marijuana fields are and pay the farmers to inform on Americans to whom they sell grass. The farmer even gets back the grass he sold you. Most Mexican farmers are good people but if you do not know your source you are taking a chance.

May the Breath of God be always upon your lips.

—M.J.S.

Good afternoon, boys and girls, welcome the Wonderful World of Dope! I'm your host, Atomic, and across the table from me you'll today's guest, *Cannabis Sativa*! Today we'll be reviewing methods of making the dope you have into superweed *twice*, *three*, or *more times as strong* as it was when purchased. We'll also cover how to make hash, hash oil, Isomerization of Cannabidiol, and sundry other items of arcane pharmacopeia.

First, the dope to be extracted from must be processed for cleanliness. If marijuana is used, the seeds should be removed, though broken seed husks may be left in, as they contain some THC and virtually none of the harsh hempseed oils. The remaining material, leaves and stems, should be broken down as small as possible, though it might be possible to leave aside the best flowering tops for a process involving them. The material to be processed can be placed in a blender, with or without a solvent, and chopped up at low spped. Use of a solvent in the chopping operation will dissolve a maximum of the soluble resins in the first step.

CHOPPA! CHURNA CHOPPA!

Hasheesh should be broken up into small granules before being broken down; again, use of a solvent is recommended, as hasheesh is frequently quite dense, and if chopped dry in a blender, may show some tendency to jam or stall the blades. If the hash is hard, it can be cut with a sharp knife heated to a dull red glow in a gas flame. It may also be shredded on a cheese grater, or heated *gently* in an oven until it begins to soften. Powdered hash should not be left exposed, as it will quickly lose it's potency.

The next step is *refluxing*, using a solvent to extract the vital resins from the matrix material. Once all of the vital principle has been extracted, the solvent is removed and the resins are isolated. This refluxing apparatus is designed to build up from common kitchen utensils and supplies easily available from any hardware store.

ICE

ONE INCH STRIPS OF RUBBE
INNER TUBE

LARGER STEW POT LID OF
WOK (WITHOUT HANDLES)

POLYETHYLENE TRASH BA

LARGE STEW POT

STAINLESS STEEL POT

ONE INCH ROPE SPACERS

SOLVENT CONTAINING CANNABIS

TWIN PLATE HOTPLATE

ASSEMBLY AND OPERATION

Position the tub securely on the hotplate and lay the rope strips inside. Then place the Large Stew Pot atop the ropes, place the Stainless Steel Pot inside the LSP and place the solvent/cannabis mash into the SSP. Secure the Larger Stew Pot Lid *or* a Stainless Steel Wok (without handles) over the LSP, then lay the Plastic Garbage Bag over the Wok (or LSPL). Fasten it tightly to the sides of the LSP with the rubber strips and force out all the air form under it with your hands. Pile much ice on the Plastic Bag over the Wok, fill the Tub halfway with water, and turn on the hotplate until the water boils. This heats the apparatus to about 212° F.

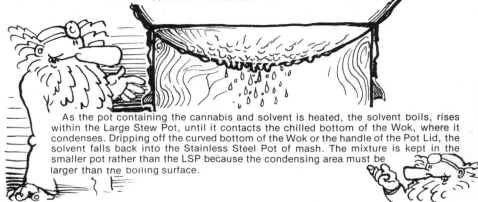

As the pot containing the cannabis and solvent is heated, the solvent boils, rises within the Large Stew Pot, until it contacts the chilled bottom of the Wok, where it condenses. Dripping off the curved bottom of the Wok or the handle of the Pot Lid, the solvent falls back into the Stainless Steel Pot of mash. The mixture is kept in the smaller pot rather than the LSP because the condensing area must be larger than the boiling surface.

138

The plastic sheeting is used for several reasons. It seals the atmosphere in the reaction vessel completely off from the external atmosphere, preventing the leakage of toxic fumes. If the plastic begins to inflate, it is a sign to the alchemist that his batch is starting to get hot inside, pressure is building up, and more ice should be placed in the Wok.

So reflux the cannabis for about three or four hours. In this period the solvent will remove all resins from the cellulose material, and will be ready for further steps.

First, however, a word on several solvents that will work in this device, their pros and cons!

Methanol or Methyl Alcohol (wood alcohol) is easily available at some pharmacies and camping goods stores, where it is sold as fuel for some portable campstoves. Care must be taken to insure pure methanol, since it is occasionally found with other substances mixed in. It is, in itself, quite poisonous, and its toxic fumes are explosive, so if it is used it must be kept totally sealed in the refluxing apparatus, and must be completely removed from the final cannabis product. Boils at 190 F (64 C).

Ethanol or Grain Alcohol, an excellent solvent, is also the active principle in Liquor, so it is heavily taxed and rather difficult to procure in pure form. Denatured spirits contain toxic substances intended to render the stuff unfit for drinking, but since these evaporate at the same temperature as the alcohol, they provide little difficulty in use as a solvent, if one makes sure that no solvent remains in the extract. Boiling point is 78.5 C.

139

Isopropyl or Rubbing Alcohol is available at drugstores and is a satisfactory solvent, though it is frequently adulterated with water. This will cause a lot on non-psychoactive tars and flavorings to be extracted as well, giving the result a bad flavor. If the extract is to be processed further, however, both the water and such tars as it brings along can be removed easily.

Petroleum Ether produces a smaller yield of extract than any alcohol, but the extract is of far greater weight-by-weight potency. It is advised that if pet ether is to be used, a prior extraction be carried out with alcohol. Thus, ,ar less of the highly explosive, toxic ether need be used to extract further. Since petroleum ether is a distillate product, its boiling temperature depends on what temperature and pressure it was cracked (fractionated) at. Pet ethers, therefore, boil over a range of temperatures, usually 30 -60 C. Ether must be ice cold when poured; some ethers will boil at room temperature.

After refluxing, the hotplate is turned off and the apparatus is allowed to cool. (See procedure on next page.) It then yields a Stainless Steel Pot containing a soupy mixture of broken-down cannabis matrix cellulose, solvent and resins. This is drained into a holding vessel, the SSP replaced in the apparatus, and a colander placed over its top, as shown. A large piece of filter paper is placed in the colander, and a strainer is placed on top of it. The solvent and mash are poured through the strainer and back into the SSP. The apparatus is set up for action as before, and the heat is turned back on.

Rather than using a strainer or filter paper, the mash can be poured through a pillowcase in the colander, tied into it, and refluxed thusly.

STRAINER

FILTER PAPER

COLANDER

The stems and cellulose are held in the strainer and filter, but they still contain a fair amount of resins. As the syrup boils, the solvent fumes condense on the chilled Wok, drip through the filter, and eventually percolate all resins into the SSP. An hour's refluxing should be sufficient.

Now it's time to remove the solvent from the extract. After seeing that the apparatus has cooled sufficiently from the filtering phase, remove the filter and the strainer containing the leached marijuana material and put it away to dry. (It is used to make hash.) Take a round cake pan somewhat wider than the SSP and place it in the colander, leaving the solvent-resin syrup in the bottom of the SSP. Enclose the apparatus, and charge with ice, as before.

To cool the apparatus after using, it may be set into a nearby tub of ice and water, which will cool it down right away. A blanket kept soaking in this tub can be used as a fire extinguisher in case trouble develops.

Heat the apparatus, and the solvent, essentially pure, will collect in the cakepan in the colander, rather than running back into the SSP. An hour or two of this operation will provide a pan of solvent and an SSP containing *crude cannabis extract*. It should contain no solvent, though it may harbor additional substances or water which it might be desirable to remove.

Store the purified solvent! It can be used in later extractions!

To remove the water that may be present in the extract, fill a large pot with cooking oil, place the SSP containing the extract into it, and clip a candy or deep-fry thermometer into the oil. If a toxic solvent has been used, place a bit of water in the extract and heat the oil to about 220 F. When a small mirror held over the SSP no longer fogs, all water will have been driven off, and all toxic chemicals as well, since they evaporate at a lower temperature.

This yields an extract (Purified Crude Cannabis Extract) which is pure enough to eat or smoke, though it still contains substances which do hot contribute to the high and can be removed from the resin.

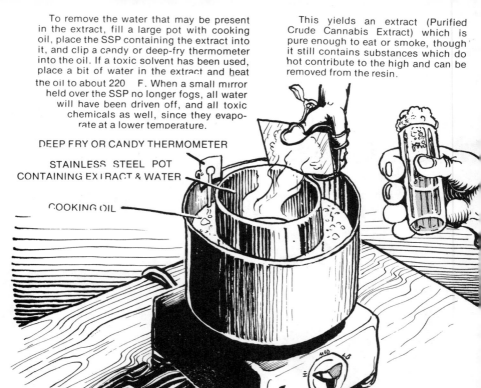

DEEP FRY OR CANDY THERMOMETER

STAINLESS STEEL POT CONTAINING EXTRACT & WATER

COOKING OIL

Dissolve the Purified Crude Cannabis extract in five times its weight of alcohol, and pour with an equal volume of water into a large jar with a screw top. See sure that the mixture is not warm. Add a volume of pet ether to half the volume of water used, tighten the cap, invert the jar, then turn upright immediately. Let the mixture run down the sides of the jar for a moment, then uncap to relieve pressure, recap the bottle, and repeat. Do this about 25 times, then let the jug sit for about a half-hour and permit the contents to settle. It will separate into distinct layers, then the below apparatus may be used to blow the ether-extract layer off the top and into a collection jar.

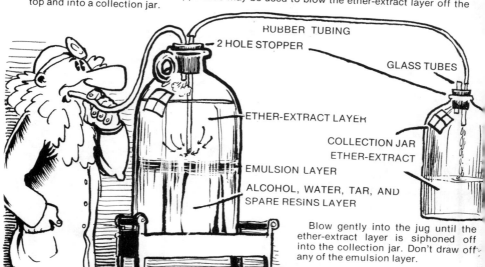

RUBBER TUBING

2 HOLE STOPPER

GLASS TUBES

ETHER-EXTRACT LAYER

COLLECTION JAR
ETHER-EXTRACT

EMULSION LAYER

ALCOHOL, WATER, TAR, AND SPARE RESINS LAYER

Blow gently into the jug until the ether-extract layer is siphoned off into the collection jar. Don't draw off any of the emulsion layer.

Add another volume of fresh pet ether and do it again, ar
the ether-extract layer is clear after settling.

Now take all of this ether-extract solution and pour it
position the colander and the cakepan on it, and put into
apparatus. Charge up with ice as before, and slowly heat t
F. After evaporating the ether save it for later use, and ¡
containing the oil into a boiling water bath for a few momer
any residual traces of ether. The yield is much reduced fr
steps, but the potency is far greater. This shall be referred to as *Purified
Cannabis Extract* and is to be differentiated from *Purified CRUDE
Cannabis Extract*

TIME HAS COME TO GET INTO SOME **LONG RUBBER GLOVES** AN'
GIT DOWN TO SOME NITTY-GRITTY CHEMISTRY! IT'S TIME TO
ISOMERIZE CANNABIDIOL INTO THC AND CONVERT
THE THC INTO AN **ISOMER** OF ITSELF WHICH IS FAR MORE POTENT!

The Purified Cannabis Extract
contains several substances which
yield the smell and taste; two
non-psychoactive chemicals (cannabinol and cannabidiol), of which
cannabidiol yields the commonly
known effect of the "munchies"; and
THC (Tetrahydrocannabinol). Naturally, the more potent the hash or
weed used is, the more potent the
extract and the higher the level of
THC. It is, however, possible to
convert the Cannabidiol into THC,
and to simultaneously alter the
low-rotating THC present to
the higher-rotating *Isomers*.

The potency of extract which has
been processed in this manner may at
least be doubled, though in some
cases it may be as much as five or six
times stronger! This method, however, involves the use of pure,
concentrated sulfuric acid, a dangerous reagent, so great care must be
exercised in the performance of the
operation.

"Rotation" refers to the indicated
double molecular bond and its position on the lefthand carbon ring. In
Cannabidiol and THC (low rot) it is in
a lower position; after isomerization
it has moved to a higher position.

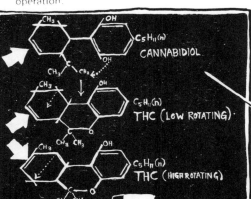

CANNABIDIOL $C_5H_{11}(n)$

THC (LOW ROTATING) $C_5H_{11}(n)$

THC (HIGH ROTATING) $C_5H_{11}(n)$

Dissolve the Purified Cannabis Extract in absolute ethanol or pure methanol in the ratio of one gram extract to ten grams solvent. There must be no water in this solution, as the next step is the addition of one drop of 100 % sulfuric acid per gram of extract. Add the acid slowly, drop by drop, stirring slowly and completely, with a long glass stirring rod.

Place a Pyrex pot containing the extract-alcohol-acid solution into the refluxing apparatus (using the Pyrex pot instead of the SSP, because of the reactive nature of the acid) and reflux for two hours. The acid will not evaporate and will remain in the Pyrex pot. Allow to cool.

Take the cooled solution, pour with an equal volume of water and ½ volume pet ether into the ether-extraction apparatus (pg. 6) and use as before. Allow to settle, blow off the ether-extract layer, and discard the water.

This leaves an ether-extract-acid mix from which the acid must be purged. To accomplish this, pour the ether-extract solution into four volumes of 5% sodium bicarbonate solution (1 gr. bicarb to 20 gr. water). This will neutralize the acid, releasing CO_2 and leaving a solution of Sodium Sulphate (Na_2SO_4). Permit this to settle into layers, then blow off the ether-extract layer, then repeat the step with pure water rather than bicarb solution. Using the SSP in the refluxing apparatus and the solvent-collection pan in the colander, separate the extract and the ether, storing ether for future work. The extract now contains a much higher percentage of THC, as determined by the amount of Cannabidiol present. All THC in this extract has been enhanced and is now the high-rotating isomeric form. All toxins have been removed from the extract.

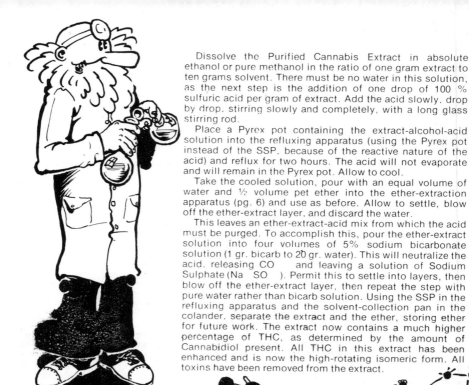

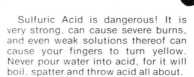

Sulfuric Acid is dangerous! It is very strong, can cause severe burns, and even weak solutions thereof can cause your fingers to turn yellow. Never pour water into acid, for it will boil, spatter and throw acid all about.

When working with Sulfuric Acid (or any caustic or corrosive), always wear safety glasses, long rubber gloves, a rubber lab apron, and clothing that covers as much of the skin as possible. A face mask is also a good idea. In case of acid burns, have a bottle of bicarb solution on hand, as much bicarb as will dissolve in the water, and dash this instantly on any acid that contacts the skin. The acid should be kept in a tightly sealed reagent bottle in a styrofoam or polyurethane-foam lined box.

Dissolve the Purified Cannabis Extract in absolute ethanol or methanol, 1 gr. extract to 10 gr. solvent.

GLICK! GLICK!

There must be no water in this solution.

Add one drop Sulfuric Acid per gram of extract.

H₂SO₄

Add acid drop-by-drop slowly, avoiding spills, spatters.

Place in Pyrex pot in Refluxing Apparatus.

Reflux 2 hours, allow to cool.

Mix solution into equivalent volume of water and ½ volume pet ether.

Follow ether extraction procedure.

Pour mixture into four volumes of water in jug, gently invert 25 times, letting off pressure between inversions.

SLOSH!

ME BIG CHEF

Siphon off ether-extract layer. Add to four volumes of 5% sodium bicarbonate solution.

SODA

Mix, let settle, and siphon off ether-extract layer.

Remove ether from extract with collection pan in colander.

Super Extract!

IK.

NT NOTHIN' BETTER'N'A HASH SANDWICH!

The making of hasheesh is an ancient art with countless variations. Many colors, flavors, consistencies, potencies and different methods of preparation exist all over the world, and since most of these are due to strictly local conditions, it's impractical to try and duplicate most natural hashes in the lab.

However, "artificial" hash can be made easily from cannabis-lab materials, and if done correctly will be indistinguishable from (and in some cases superior to) imported hasheesh.

Take a volume of pure *Isomerized Super-extract* and heat it until it flows smoothly, then pour into a mortar with dried, powdered deactivated cannabis material. Grind the two together until the mixture is homogenous, then add more powder until the desired texture is arrived at.

Knead it with your fingers.

·One can also roll many tiny hashballs, then roll them in the dried powder, and loosely force them together, like a snowball. Put aside in a cool, slightly moist, humidor to age, this hash will be dark, spongy and have superlative burning qualities due to its porosity. A similar hash can be made by piling many thin layers of hash upon one another, separated by layers of cannabis dust.

Roll it out on a sheet of waxed paper. It can be rolled into worms, turds, balls; or rolled out beneath a rolling pin into wafers, slabs, thin sheets.

147

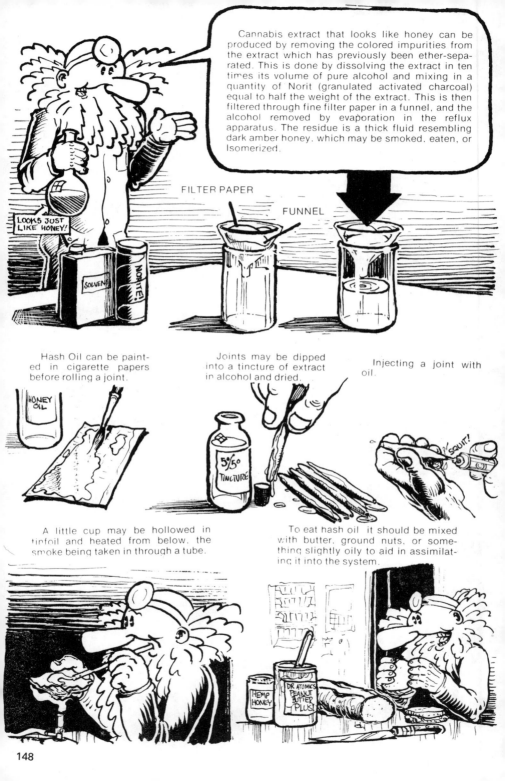

Cannabis extract that looks like honey can be produced by removing the colored impurities from the extract which has previously been ether-separated. This is done by dissolving the extract in ten times its volume of pure alcohol and mixing in a quantity of Norit (granulated activated charcoal) equal to half the weight of the extract. This is then filtered through fine filter paper in a funnel, and the alcohol removed by evaporation in the reflux apparatus. The residue is a thick fluid resembling dark amber honey. which may be smoked. eaten, or Isomerized.

LOOKS JUST LIKE HONEY!

SOLVENT NORITE!

FILTER PAPER

FUNNEL

Hash Oil can be painted in cigarette papers before rolling a joint.

HONEY OIL

Joints may be dipped into a tincture of extract in alcohol and dried.

5%50 TINCTURE

Injecting a joint with oil.

SQUIT!

A little cup may be hollowed in tinfoil and heated from below. the smoke being taken in through a tube.

To eat hash oil it should be mixed with butter. ground nuts, or something slightly oily to aid in assimilating it into the system.

HEMP HONEY

DR ATOMIC'S PEANUT BUTTER PLUS!

1 lb. Reg
$150-200

Reflux

Isomerize

1 lb. hash worth
$600-1000

Prepare Hash

Isomerize

1 kilo Reg
$200-350

Separate ½ lb. flowering tops and
reflux in cheesecloth bags.

Reflux everything else.

Flowers - $300,
Hash - $600-1000

Prepare 1 lb. hash,
½ lb. superflowers.

Reduce and Isomerize.

1 lb. low grade domestic weed
$50-100/lb.

Tops bagged and refluxed

Extract reduced

Superweed worth
$350-400/lb.

Resaturated into tops

Isomerized

149

Reflux and Reduce

Isomerize

3-5 oz. Super Extract
worth $500/oz.

Owing as to periodic fluctuations in the price of both domestic and imported commodities, the above figures can only be considered approximate. However, there is enough give and take in the variability of plant yield to make for some profit in any operation. There is a particularly high markup for pure honey oil, for example, such that the given $300 worth of weed can yield up to $1500 worth of oil.

BOOKS FOR REFERENCE

CONNOISSEUR'S HANDBOOK OF MARIJUANA
   by William Daniel Drake Jr.
   San Francisco, Straight Arrow Books, 1971
CANNABIS ALCHEMY, THE ART OF MODERN HASHMAKING
   by David Hoye
   San Francisco. Level Press, 1973
MARIJUANA CONSUMER'S AND DEALER'S GUIDE
   by Mary Jane Superweed
   San Francisco, Stone Kingdom, 1968
SUPER GRASS GROWER'S GUIDE
   by Mary Jane Superweed
   San Francisco, Stone Kingdom, 1971
PHARMACEUTICAL STUDY OF CANNABIS
(BEING A COLLATION OF FACTS AS KNOWN AT PRESENT DATE)
   by E. Whimeray
   EQUINOX MAGAZINE, Vol 1, #1, 1909
   Reprinted in
HASHEESH, THE HERB DANGEROUS
   edited by David Hoye
   San Francisco, Level Press, 1973
RECENT DEVELOPMENTS IN CANNABIS CHEMISTRY
   by Alexander T. Shulgin, Ph.D
   JOURNAL OF PSYCHEDELIC DRUGS, Vol 2, #1, 1971
Papers of Roger Adams
   JOURNAL OF THE AMERICAN CHEMICAL SOCIETY,
   Pg. 196. Vol 62, 1940
   JOURNAL OF THE AMERICAN CHEMICAL SOCIETY,
   Pg. 2211. Vol 63, 1941